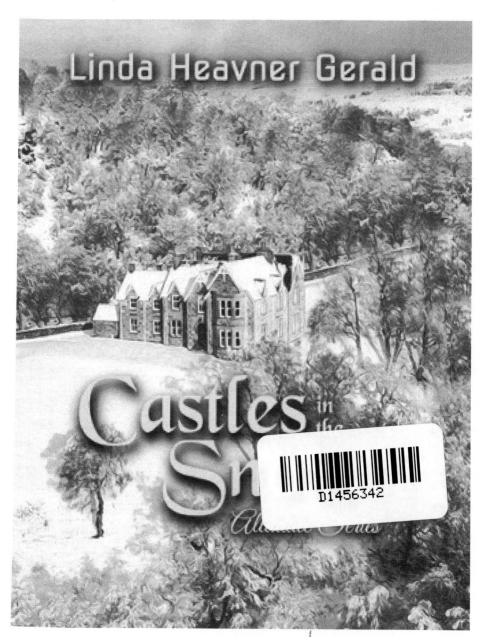

Linda Heavner Gerald

Castles in the Snow

Atlantic Series

Linda Heavner Gerald

Published by Lime Pie Publishing

Port St. Joe, Florida 32457

All rights reserved.

Published in the United States of America

Manufactured in the United States of America

First Edition

ISBN 13: 9798645758141

Other Works by Linda Heavner Gerald

Betrayed in Beaufort

Rosemary's Beach House

Dusty the Island Dog

Cycles of Hatred

Till Heaven Then Forever

Confessions of an Assassin

Sins of Summer

Murdered Twice

Enchanted

I Am Red

Claire's House

The Soldier and the Author

AnnaPolis Summers

VieVie LaFontaine

Dear John

Table 36

Perfect

Castles in the Snow

Dedication

Castles in the Snow is dedicated to our friend, Paul Lister, a deep ecologist and the founder of the 23,000 acres Alladale Wilderness Reserve and The European Nature Trust. Paul's goal is to create a controlled wolf reserve in the Highlands of Scotland.

ACKNOWLEDGMENTS

I am grateful to Paul Lister and all of the entrepreneurs who work tirelessly to pursue their goals while helping our planet, each in their way. Paul works tirelessly in his goal of demonstrating the importance of our ecosystem and our daily choice to either aid or damage it.

I want to thank Sharon K. Garner, my editor, for her guidance. Thanks also to Nicole Harmon for the extra set of eyes.

As usual, Thank You, Rob, the creative director at sales@selfpubbookcovers.com for a beautiful cover.

Linda Heavner Gerald

A Message From Paul Lister

My thoughts remain with the communities and individuals, including healthcare workers and first responders, most deeply affected by the COVID-19 crisis. Congratulations to Captain Thomas Moore on an incredible initiative, what a legacy he has created.

Nature's Red Card.

Human society has reached a tipping point, and it's time for all of us to take a good look in the mirror. Albert Einstein once said: "the definition of insanity is doing the same thing over and over again, but expecting different results." The wave we have been riding has now crashed ashore, and each of us will be required to change habits and make new choices in all aspects of our lives. None of us are exempt, nor will we be unaffected by the consequences of inaction; the alternative could well be an extinction-level event.

Regardless of personal opinions or the latest conspiracy theory, we now know COVID-19 is not going anywhere fast. This deeply egalitarian virus affects all of us, regardless of religion, fitness, class, colour, ethnicity, affluence, age or sexual orientation. There is no doubt that our abuse of the environment lies at the root, or has at least contributed towards the virus's manifestation, and we must also take responsibility for it spreading to all four corners of the planet.

Environmental destruction is fueled by our seemingly insatiable appetite for non-essential goods and services, propelled by massive advertising and marketing campaigns. Over the lifetimes of Queen Elizabeth II and Sir David Attenborough, the global population has quadrupled. This, combined with an ever-increasing amount of consumption, has led to a terminal drain on natural resources, pollution, famine, unemployment, global poverty, climate change and the rising tide and natural disasters, such as the devastating fires in USA, Brazil and Australia. It was recently calculated that humanity needs 1.7 earths to sustain almost 8-billion of us; failure to take population into account when trying to analyse the challenges we face is to ignore the elephant in the room.

We need to seriously challenge the capital growth model and realise the consequences of such behaviour. The plant, fungal and non-human animal kingdom lives within a well-balanced 'trophic cascade'. Humanity, on the other hand, has carved up the world into countries with political and religious polarities that make it nearly impossible to reach consensus on issues that threaten our existence.

It pains me to see the overwhelming sprawl of degraded, over-farmed and over-grazed lands throughout Europe that were once 'living landscapes', full of forests, wetlands, peatlands and grasslands, teeming with wildlife and acting as a mega carbon store. These utopias, other than the steep slopes and remote valleys of the Carpathians, Alps and other small pockets, are now transformed into bleak, sanitised, 'industrial style' mega-farms;

interrupted only by urban development, complete with homes, apartment blocks, shopping centres, factories, offices and warehouses. This is not exclusive to Europe; wild lands, from North America and Africa to Brazil and Indonesia, have been logged and burnt to make way for extensive agricultural development. Unbelievably, a massive 27% of the world's entire landmass (excluding ice caps and deserts) has been cleared for livestock farming (in many cases heavily subsidised) and associated feed crops. The fashion, textile, disposable furniture and mining industries are also responsible for excessive deforestation.

I have some personal insight into these industries. In 1964, my father co-founded the MFI retail business, which grew to become the UK's largest furniture retailer over 20 years. In 1985, he sold his remaining interest in the company and was excited to transition from entrepreneur to philanthropist by establishing the United Kingdom Sailing Academy (UKSA). Meanwhile, I continued for a further 15 years in the furniture business, which came to an abrupt halt when Dad suffered a severe stroke and I took several months away from the office to be with him in hospital and support Mum.

During this difficult period of my life, I had the opportunity to reflect and realise I was part of the problem; so I decided to exit the 'low-cost, fast furniture' business and move into the world of conservation. I established The European Nature Trust (TENT) to support a variety of conservation and wildlife initiatives. In 2003, I purchased Alladale in Scotland to embark on a re-wilding programme and the creation of a wilderness reserve, as opposed to the hunting, shooting and fishing land-management model. This has resulted in a much healthier and more biodiverse landscape, with a greater variety of tourists now visiting the area. It has been a real privilege to dedicate my time and resources towards restoring natural habitats and fighting for environmental causes.

Whilst filming a BBC documentary in Argentina in 2007, I had the good fortune to meet and become close friends with Doug and Kris Tompkins, environmentalists who decided to "sell up"their interests in the hugely successful clothing brands Esprit, North Face and Patagonia and focus on their passion for wild land restoration. This inspirational couple have become the world's greatest philanthropic conservationists, in my opinion. Over the last 25 years, their projects in Chile and Argentina have led to the creation and protection of 10 million acres of national parks. Doug used to share with me his feelings of guilt over the fashion brands he created; he also told me of the endless debates he had with Steve Jobs. One constant theme struck a chord: Steve would argue that technology will come to humanity's rescue, whilst Doug maintained that nature and beauty will be our saviour. Perhaps both are true. Let's look at some of the challenges we face and decide.

Surely we should begin to legislate for the greater good, rather than allowing society to put money above the welfare of future generations? Politicians, financiers, business leaders and the capital markets are of the belief that the planet can supply a burgeoning population with infinite resources to fuel the global economy. I refer to this ideal as the 'never-ending exponential growth monster'. With the offers of interest-free loans, combined with aggressive advertising campaigns, we are incentivised to buy more and more things we don't actually need: another home upgrade, a new kitchen or sofa, the latest fashion items, disposable plastic toys, low-cost flights, the newest electric car — or yet another smartphone. We must acknowledge the carbon impact of unnecessary and excessive trading of goods like cars and wine that crisscross the oceans filling carriers and containers!

The UN suggests that the world population is currently growing at a rate of approximately 81 million people each year; looking at the facts objectively, I think most of us can agree the planet will not be able to sustain this growth. This scenario looms ahead of us with the inevitability of an oncoming freight train. There are, of course, many contributing reasons for the sharp rise in global population, from religion, poverty, poor education, financial incentives, disease and cultural beliefs, amongst others. I hear a lot of people pass the blame and say, "Oh, but the average family in Europe and North America have less than two kids and the issue lies with developing regions like Africa, India and South-east Asia." Whilst it's true that the majority of population growth occurs in these regions, the overall burden of consumption and carbon emissions of a person living in the developed world is up to 150 times that of an individual living in the undeveloped world — the very places that are most affected by climate change.

Whilst efforts such as recycling, mitigating the use of plastics, installing solar panels and the purchase of an electric vehicle are well-intentioned, we must accept the fact that infinite growth on a finite planet is not an option; less is definitely more. We must now dramatically reduce our consumption, whilst simultaneously tackling the herd of elephants in the room — the population problem. Against our emotional instincts, we need to consider a one-woman, one-child policy (with adoption as an option for a second child) and accept the short/medium-term issues that might prevail. Alternatively, we might well follow a similar path of the Mayan civilisation: deforestation, excessive cultivation, climate change, drought, crop failure, famine and, finally, starvation. This is not an easy or popular thing to say, but we have reached a crossroads in our evolution and we must take these issues seriously. If we don't, it will be nothing short of catastrophic.

Prior to Covid-19, we became accustomed to a daily scourge of holiday offers along with relentless discounts from low-cost operators. There are the cruise ship holidays to Antarctica: quite possibly the most remote, inhospitable, and unspoiled place on earth; probably best left to the scientists and researchers to measure the effects of climate change on the ice! After all, thanks to Sir David, we have the opportunity to watch the most amazing natural history films, with incredible landscape and wildlife sequences, without leaving our home.

Similarly, despite the extensive breadth and depth of online and TV sports coverage, millions of people — at a personal and carbon cost — jump in cars, hop on trains or book a flight to attend away matches and games. The 2019 UEFA Europa League final between Chelsea and Arsenal was played in Baku (Azerbaijan), thousands of air miles from London. Why was the match not played at Wembley, for example? Just imagine the negative impacts of motorsports, polo and international horse racing, with the air freighting of cars and stressed horses around the globe! Is it clever or justifiable to host weddings, stag and hen parties abroad, so all guests are required to fly at their own expense and that of the environment? What about non-essential educational exchanges, where graduates and parents opt for schooling overseas, plus the additional carbon cost for visiting family and friends?

We must look at the traditional definition of 'achievement', which pertains to material success and the accomplishments of talented entrepreneurs, sports stars, artists and celebrities. The top 1% of wealthiest people control 45% of the world's capital; how sustainable can this be in light of current circumstances? Successful entrepreneurs and global celebrities represent a tiny minority of the population, while most people are employed or operate modest businesses. However, creating and leaving a 'legacy' is a very different matter. In my view, a legacy is related to contribution and charitable giving, moving beyond endless wealth creation.

We all know how celebrity 'aura' can empower, bringing focus and funding to good causes (such as we have witnessed with the current pandemic). To give money is one thing, but to get involved and roll your sleeves up is so much more rewarding and effective, especially with such a pool of global talent. But here comes the crunch: less than 3% of charitable giving is directed towards the environment, climate change, and wildlife. One must remember, we depend on nature — nature does not depend on us. As the Scottish-American naturalist and adventurer, John Muir, wrote, "When one tugs at a single thing in nature, he finds it attached to the rest of the world".

So what else can we do to avoid the bleak future that is thundering towards us like the four horsemen of the apocalypse?

Surely, it's time for us all to move towards a plant-based diet for a richer and more sustainable environment? Shifting from the horrendous factory- and industrial-scale farms, filled with suffering livestock, would improve carbon capture, mitigate flooding and help prevent droughts. It might create cleaner air, reduce contaminated water and lead to healthier soils — the very fabric of all life on earth. Over time, agricultural areas could be re-wilded, thereby increasing recreational spaces for burgeoning urban dwellers, whilst allowing rural communities to engage with an agro-economy, based on nature tourism and associated micro industries. We should also understand that zoonotic diseases like SARS, Bird Flu and Covid-19 are the direct result of our proximity to livestock, domesticated and wild animals. David Quammen, scientist and author of Spillover: Animal Infections and the Next Human Pandemic writes, "Humanity is a kind of animal, inextricably connected with other animals: in origin and in descent, in sickness and in health."

We also need to pay closer attention to where our produce comes from: green beans from New Zealand, garlic from China, apples from Chile, grapes air-freighted from South Africa, Spanish tomatoes, Argentinian and Californian wines, water from Fiji, vegetables, fruits and kelp from Australia and beer from Japan. We need to consider the toxic industry of flying decorative flowers from Colombia and East Africa to Holland, only to be then redistributed all over Europe. With extended supply chains already under pressure, local produce for local communities is a mantra we must heed with a move towards an 'eco-localism' model. This can even extend to our own green spaces. Wild gardens, which have proved so popular at shows, can support a huge amount of flora and fauna, encouraging bees and other essential pollinators. Even better, explore the principles of permaculture and plant some vegetables too. Replacing traditional lawns in this way would not only save on mower fuels and harmful pesticides, but mitigate further the carbon footprint associated with food production whilst reducing your GMO intake.

As a result of Covid-19, the travel industry will be impacted for months and years to come, which means responsible, conscious and sustainable travel will be the new norm. During lockdown, we have become used to holding meetings via Zoom, Skype, WhatsApp and other applications, challenging the need for wasteful and unnecessary business trips. There has never been a more compelling reason for a 'stay-cation' to explore corners of the UK you hadn't considered before, helping support the struggling hospitality industry and the people whose livelihoods depend on it. When international travel becomes possible, why not spend time connecting with the wilder areas of Europe, from the Carpathians and Asturias to Abruzzo and Scandinavia? Wherever we live, let's prove our worth by making compassionate and discerning choices and enjoying the treasures of our continent. Further afield, a well-researched African or Indian wildlife trip can go a long way in supporting local communities, protecting wildlife and helping to combat illegal poaching.

Finally, one of humanity's unique traits is that no two people think alike; therefore, I trust you realise these are my personal opinions, which will not be shared by all. However, at the very least, I hope you'll take time to reflect on the changes you can make toward a more harmonious world when we emerge from lockdown. We can all do something, and there is no time to waste.

Best wishes and stay healthy,

Paul

References: www.ourworldindata.org
https://www.yesmagazine.org/video/coronavirus-pandemic-arundhati-roy/

Prologue

The scent of fresh heather soothed my agitated spirit when I opened my eyes. That familiar herb-like smell calmed me. A pretty blue pot sat on a table beside my bed. It contained the heather's tiny cup-shaped, pink-purple flowers. Their beauty made me smile —a memory of long ago rushed into my head.

Many blurred images in my head matched the haziness of my vision. The room appeared familiar, but the circumstances were foreign. *Why are tiny pellets of ice hitting my eyes? Is that the reason I can't see things well?* Something felt terribly wrong. Again, I closed my eyes. Forcing them together accomplished nothing but more fog.

###

I stood with him, my beloved Thomas, atop a snow-covered hill. A stately Victorian lodge smiled at us from the white top across the way.

"Alladale?" I whispered the name as the image of the sprawling manor home filled my senses. It was as though I was seeing her for the first time. "My Love! That is Alladale? I had begun to doubt her existence."

Those words I now repeated as I had five years earlier. How often have I thought about this moment in time? I wondered.

When I had looked so long ago at the tall, blond man with chiseled good looks standing beside me, I recognized how blessed I was. Yes, we had suffered the painful blows of life but still stood together. Alladale, Thomas, and I, those three remained a given.

My gaze now darted around the room.

"What is this place?" My words were a mere whisper.

Then I knew. *This place is my favorite room in the mansion, the Willow Suite. Does this mean that my brain is functioning? At least a part of me is well?*

The color of the heather matched that of the spread covering the generous bed. I reached out to touch the satiny smoothness, which looked familiar, but I couldn't. Someone had shackled my hands. No panic assailed me from this realization. I breathed deeply.

Yes, that is the pleasing scent of heather. With longing, I reached toward the blooms, but the shackles on my wrists prevented me.

"Thomas, I don't understand! Where are you? Who has done this to me?"

Once again, I looked around, trying to figure out what was going on. *Why would my husband leave me shackled to the bed?* I wondered. Intense pain engulfed my arms and legs as well as my head. Perhaps a head injury had resulted in my damaged vision and the tenderness I was experiencing? I closed my eyes.

When I woke, it dawned on me that my surroundings felt comfortable. A blazing fire roared in the massive old fireplace in the room. The heat felt too intense. I wished that I could lower the pink-purple spread but remembered that the window above my bed gaped open. *That's the reason for the stinging pellets of ice.*

Although the opening looked small, eventually, as the fire diminished, the temperature would plummet. I struggled to free myself, even though I was certain it was impossible.

A large white pitcher, which contained a small chip, sat beside the pretty blue pot of flowers. For the first time, I felt thirsty. This sensation frightened me.

How much worse will it become? Will I realize each moment as I die from dehydration, starvation, or cold? What about relieving myself? My struggling accomplished nothing. My only choice was to wait. *Thomas will return soon, I'm sure of it. Always, he has been my savior.*

Like horses charging from captivity, memories abruptly trampled my mind, those of Thom, me, Max, and others. My parents? I smiled, but those fast-moving recollections arrived too quickly; they confused me. It was impossible to figure out what was happening now in the present. *I must examine each thought!* The realization that taking pleasure in them would occupy my time, thus keeping me from experiencing the terror I knew waited. If, instead, I fought to recall the pleasant thoughts, starting with my first memory of my husband, maybe my sanity would be prolonged? *Now, what is my first memory?*

For a second time, I smiled. Another house, located in a different place, floated into my mind. It wasn't Alladale. This other place was also precious to me. Grappling with a long-ago event in my life, I reminisced, "Charleston, my childhood home in the United States."

My words trickled into the heavy air, reinforcing my desire to examine every memory from my past—especially those involving my husband. Each vital moment of my life concerned him. I snuggled under the spread while I tussled with many recollections.

This story is my life: mine, and that of Thomas Baxter Reid. Our tapestry of frayed ends would now knit themselves into lovely protection from the lonely agony I faced.

"Am I dying?"

But the only thing that mattered to me was his safety.

Chapter One

"Caroline Emma Corbett, whatever happens here, will not be pleasant. Someone intends you terrible harm, even death. You must not panic. If you have any chance of survival, then you must stay calm." I hurled those words into the overheated room.

The atmosphere was unpleasant; my body glistened with perspiration. I realized that if my captor didn't return soon, the opposite sensation, freezing temperatures, would be my end. *How long can a person live without food and water?* I asked myself.

A research paper that I had written in college for a writing class now proved helpful as I recalled that a person could survive only three to four days without water but up to three weeks without food. I stared at the pretty white pitcher with a chip in the top and wondered if it really contained water or if it was meant to drive me insane as I begged for relief? Strangely, I recognized the pitcher and wondered how it was chipped.

"Okay, stop it right now! If you're going to survive this, and your odds aren't great, you have to remain focused." Once more, like a madwoman, I ranted to myself.

"How can I be calm with my hands shackled to this bed? And I'm alone, without food or water. Hello! Is anyone here? Can you hear me? Please, I need help! PLEASE!"

Only the roar of the fire and the wind from the open window replied. *And why was the window left open?* None of this made sense. *Who would start a roaring fire but leave the window above the bed ajar?* My gaze scoured the room for clues. There weren't any. Ice pellets continued to hit my eyes as the wind blew them angrily onto my face. They began to annoy me.

As if in answer to my exhausting questions, I fell deeply asleep. My mind told me to concentrate on my past. *Maybe I should trace my life, taking stock of mostly happy things, but those will surely stir up the not-so-pleasant recollections.* With this plan, my awareness became dreams; most of my beloved husband, Thomas.

"Thom are you still alive?" I heard myself mumble those words but was unable to answer.

My other persistent thought was of the beautiful wedding-cake house where I grew up in Charleston, South Carolina. I had never considered the similarities between Scotland, my adopted home, and South Carolina until Thomas declared that we must move from South Carolina to Scotland upon his college graduation. He assured me that other than the stifling summers of Charleston, they were very similar. I had never heard such a comparison, but the idea of avoiding the heat appealed to me. I had never taken well to the long, hot days of the South.

Early in our lives, this man who I loved had gone mad with the history of the Reid Clan. I had helped him the summer before he left for college, and we pored over ancestral websites. Until he began his education in architecture, he was obsessed with ancestry and Scotland. I thought about my husband's graduation from Rice University in Houston, Texas. He had refused to leave the South, but he wanted an excellent education in architecture, so he chose Rice. The university had an impeccable reputation for turning out the best.

William Marsh Rice University, named for an American businessman who left his fortune to this great institute of higher learning, remained a comprehensive research facility. It opened in 1923 after the murder of its namesake. The college's goal is to "advance tomorrow's leaders and encourage future thinkers." The Wall Street Journal rated it as "number seven in the top schools for resources." This campus of three hundred acres consistently was ranked as "one of the top twenty universities by the United States news." Another honor recently bestowed on the education pioneer in Houston, Texas, was being labeled "the second most international university." Perhaps Thom had met many Scots behind those rose-colored walls because he was changed by studying there. I believed his experience with students from the international scene gave him the confidence to move to Europe.

Such an innovative school offered fifty undergraduate majors across six divisions of study. Thomas often stressed that although he received acceptance to several Ivy League institutions, he had chosen Rice because of the School of Architecture. Rice was famous for the many notable creators of the building process who had graduated from those shiny halls. One of their exceptional requirements was for students to complete twelve hours each in the fields of humanities, social sciences, and applied sciences. Those who graduated appeared to be exceptionally well-rounded individuals. Thom sure was. He boasted about the two dozen Marshall Scholars and a dozen Rhodes Scholars who were alumni.

Two proud alumni won the Nobel Prize. I dreamed that my husband might, but it was not to be.

With such a sterling education, he should have prospered and enjoyed a life of fame in his chosen field, but the lies of my Uncle Robert had dealt him a hard blow. When his sterling reputation hung around him, "Aye, sort of like these shackles that hold me," I said aloud. We walked away from our storied lives to a new country. Both of us loved Scotland, but, right now, I was a bit confused.

I took writing classes at The College of Charleston while we remained apart, which proved to be the hardest time of my life. My mind pulled that thought from my consciousness without help. There were many reasons for my choice of higher education. I, too, could have gone Ivy League, but I didn't want to leave the local fame and fortune I enjoyed in Charleston. Everyone knew my family. I received a little special recognition because of them. Call me spoiled, but I'm not crazy. Never would I want to leave my perks for a place where no one knew me until Thomas prevailed.

The College of Charleston, I still see her grand façade, which stood with such "Southern-ness." If there was ever a grand Southern dame, it was she. Founded in 1770 and chartered in 1785, this was the first college in South Carolina and the thirteenth oldest in the United States. That's an awesome fact to those who love history, like Thomas and me. Our love for the ancient may be another attraction to Scotland.

The six large white columns that flanked her entrance always made me consider all the great thinkers who attended the College of Charleston before me. Upon graduation, I nobly carried a

Master of Fine Arts in Creative Writing across town to my stately home in The Battery. My love for all things Charleston was so great that I couldn't leave her for a mere diploma.

Honestly, I considered not going to college. My love of writing had been a part of me for so long. I had my particular style, and I sure didn't need the money, but I needed to use the time Thomas was away to benefit myself and not waste precious moments. I will forever be grateful for the education and experience of this exemplary school of higher learning. Plus, I was allowed to remain in my "city of dreams."

Thomas's brother, Max, and Max's girlfriend, Elizabeth Eisenhour, also attended with me. Max earned a degree in law. Today, he is one of the brightest and highest-paid attorneys in South Carolina. Elizabeth and I both are proud of our writing. Frequently, before I moved to Scotland, we hosted book signings together at the local stores. The bond that formed among the three of us saved my life when I became older. Their love prevented me from ever feeling lonely or living alone.

Speaking of older, I now considered my past. My heritage was well-documented in the annals of Charlestonian history, as were those of Thomas. I didn't need to spend hours investigating my roots. A family member researched all that information years earlier so that the Corbett family women might obtain membership in one of the most illustrious organizations in the United States. My membership in the DAR (Daughters of the American Revolution) filled my need for any ancient links. For as long as I could remember, the women in my family attended meetings and developed a proud bond with this prominent group.

When Thomas began to question me about my ancestors, I found his interest fascinating and offered to help him discover his past. For many years, we worked on tracing his bloodline, which we found began in Aberdeenshire (Gaelic: Siorrachd Ober Dheathain); this was in the Aberdeen area of northwestern Scotland. The Clan Reid name surfaced in historical documents before the fourteenth century. It was officially a sept of the Clan Robertson. Upon discovering all of this, he was hooked, even developing a fondness for the Gaelic language. He became proficient at speaking and reading while I always struggled with it. Frequently, in the evenings, we listened to Scottish music with the bagpipe and fiddle. I had grown fond of it. My love often danced what he described as a jig, but I had my doubts. He was great at many things, but dancing wasn't one of them.

For a while, I was happy knowing my patriot ancestor, who fought in the Revolutionary War. My noble family member had allowed me entrance into a sisterhood that I loved. Often I visited the grave of this family member, where a tall stone obelisk stood proudly in Charleston's private cemetery. Thomas sometimes accompanied me, and we laid flowers on the grave of a hero. Such pride consumed me.

At that point, I didn't understand Thom's obsession with locating ancient documents from his past. When I assisted him while he dug in dusty old journals, I thought, *Why not join him? How much farther might I trace my family links?* What I discovered was much more than ties to Britain; I located my clan, the Corbetts' history.

Castles in the Snow

My family hailed from the Normandy area of France. Their illustrious story kept me digging deep into the night for additional information. The knowledge we gleaned changed both of us. I realized our calling was more than someday raising exemplary children, which was a commendable calling, but we felt compelled to assist in a global way. We longed to accomplish greatness by educating others about the impact of ecology and conservation on our struggling planet.

While Thomas proudly studied his past, I discovered that the Corbett ancestry, thanks to Thomas's quest, was more complex than his. He worked hard during the day in his sleek new architectural office while we pored over countless websites involving ancestry in the evenings. Most days, I worked on developing my latest novel. As a couple, we prepared ourselves for a future time when we might relocate to another land—a place that held our beginnings. As we discovered bits and pieces from our research, we became emboldened to move to a new location away from our beloved South.

My husband became obsessed with everything Scottish as he longed to understand the illustrious history of his Reid Clan, so did I. Before long, he began to talk about the memorable past of this great land from which he hailed. Constantly, he researched a nation that had stolen his heart. He spoke of an earlier time when wolves ran free, while he pined for the extinct lines, and there were many. Our hearts shattered when we became aware of our land's broken environment and the damage executed to it in the name of "progress."

Thomas spoke of Britain, which was once largely and magnificently forested. "So, this is progress?" he asked.

"Can you imagine a Scotland where large carnivores, such as wolves, bears, and lynx, roam in a protected area? One where those species can't be a danger to residents? What if we, Thomas Baxter Reid, and the belle of Charleston, Caroline Emma Corbett Reid, moved there and started a nature reserve, one that provided excellent facilities?

"We could even build a lodge or two and offer patrons a chance to experience a rich environment. Maybe people could walk on nature trails and enjoy pristine waters around beautiful lakes? Those lakes could be well-stocked with brown trout and other desirable species. Can you imagine restocking Scotland with the animals that died because of the deforestation of the countryside?

"What good is all of the crops and livestock if we killed innocent, beloved animals and ruined our planet? I'm particularly interested in the reintroduction of the wolf. Is that even possible? They disappeared from the record in the early 1700s in Scotland. Can we offer a wild and raw place and support endangered species so that we can slowly create a fenced/controlled wolf reserve? It would probably resemble Romania today. If only we might initiate a plan to transport the Scottish wildcat and wolf, I would be happy." His dark eyes sparkled as he spoke. It was apparent to me that if he was to find happiness, we must move to Scotland. Our ties with our country would remain, but for a while, we must follow our hearts.

"Couldn't we just move to our beloved Cape San Blas in Florida? It sure would be easier. We both loved it there."

"What? Caroline, what are you rambling about?" He appeared confused.

"Don't you remember when I saw the large American black bear? He was huge. They have coyotes, bears, wild boars, and alligators, just to mention a few. Think of that! The Cape has black bears, but Scotland doesn't."

I realized my argument for remaining in the US was meager, but I had to try. How could I leave everyone and everything, even my country, without offering resistance?

The last time we went to Cape San Blas in Florida, with Max and Elizabeth Eisenhour, who was now his wife, before departing for college, came to mind. Thom and I had spent hours in our kayak. Often, we found ourselves surrounded by a pod of dolphins. It was magical watching them swim so close to us. It felt like I could lean over and touch them. Of course, I wouldn't do that. Never would I take a chance of harming one of those magnificent creatures. The sounds they made as they breathed filled my dreams.

I tried to picture this new land that my love championed. Frequently, he described a place with snowy mountains and the clear water of an ocean where dolphins and whales played in protected waters, surrounded by people who loved and supported them. I remembered his earlier dreams of a magical land where animals surrounded us. Was our mission in life to protect those majestic creatures who longed for human companionship?

One night, while the four of us summered on the Cape, the incident mentioned above occurred. We had enjoyed an especially exquisite meal from chef. We all felt festive. Before retiring to bed,

I noticed a trash bag that she forgot to deposit in the outside garbage container. Since the others had already gone to their rooms, I grabbed it. As I hurried outside, I heard strange sounds, grunting, and growling. *Are Thomas and my brother-in-law Max playing a trick on me?*

"Okay, guys, this is funny. I know it's you, so don't act silly." I continued toward the garbage can and saw a large, hairy form. *They'll go to any length to torment me!* Again, I laughed loudly. To my amazement, a large, well-fed black bear turned to face me. He didn't appear to be afraid of me. Instead, he just lumbered away. He never even turned around to give me a second look. I threw down the bag and scurried back inside. I phoned our chef in a panic.

"Oh, him, that's the local American black bear. He won't hurt you. In fact, he's kind of domesticated, although I wouldn't try to be too chummy. I hope you didn't throw the bag on the ground. You'll have a mess waiting for you tomorrow! Most of us have bear locks on our trash bins to avoid his rummaging. That may be something you want to consider; good night, great evening!" The phone clicked.

Yes, I had thought. *Cape characters are eccentric, as are those in Charleston. But what about the good people of Scotland? They also sound extraordinary.* I laughed as I considered kilts, bagpipes, haggis, neeps, and tatties. What awaited me if we ever made this move? The more time that passed, the more questions and excitement filled me.

Dearest Scotland, my beloved, you may take the prize for eccentricity after all. I had envisioned Thomas standing before me dressed in his cherished kilt. I heard the distant whine of bagpipes. Surely something was at play. We appeared destined to head to an unknown land because of his dreams.

As my husband worked to establish a solid architectural education elsewhere, inside my fair coastal town of salty breezes and perfect mansions, I realized that life as I knew it would change soon enough.

Upon his graduation from university, we were married in my Methodist church. Our wedding was a lavish, formal affair. That early spring evening of June 6 produced perfect weather for the wedding called "The Wedding of the Century" by The Post and Courier. Excitement had surrounded our two families as the dreams of Caroline Emma Corbett and Thomas Baxter Reid blossomed.

I had been embarrassed by the lengthy article on our extravagant celebration, but both of our families were well-connected and highly successful. Max, Thomas's older brother, had married his love, Elizabeth Eisenhour, a year earlier. Thom and I wanted Jack, their firstborn, to walk down the aisle with us, but he was too young. Our church filled with friends and family members.

That special day was beyond my wildest dreams. Max stood beside his brother. The two weren't just handsome; they were breathtaking. With significant struggles, together, we wrote our vows and proclaimed our love to each other in Gaelic, mentioning the land we dreamed of discovering. Our tie to the ageless history of glens and Caledonian pine forests stirred our very souls.

Our clan Coat of Arms, the Reid and Corbett families' emblems, proudly hung inside our new historic home near The Battery of

Charleston. We had grown up side-by-side; I in a wedding-cake house and Thom in a house of gold. Both places were beloved in that city on The Battery.

As I pondered the Corbett emblem, which featured a black crow, I told Thom that it was more interesting than the Reid Clan's red-colored one, which denoted red hair and a ruddy complexion. Max fit that mold to perfection with his shining copper hair. My love's appearance, as in all things, was different. His blond hair and chocolate eyes allowed him the possibility of hailing from several places. We found mention of Vikings and pirates in secret documents of his antiquity. My husband even purchased a kilt, which was not so strange in Charleston due to a heavy Scottish influence in the first days of the Charleston settlements; a strong bond still existed between Charleston, South Carolina, and the land we had yet to visit. Frequently, Thom began to sport the kilt to the local restaurants.

Many of the early settlers of Charleston were of Scots-Irish descent. They traveled from northern New England and Mid-Atlantic states, such as Pennsylvania. They possessed a particular ruggedness due to years of religious persecution they had suffered in Scotland and Ireland. My husband carried himself well with his muscular body. He also appeared rugged.

During the Revolutionary War, when my family's patriot was killed, American soldiers bravely fought for freedom. They took part in every battle that was fought within South Carolina. Due to their bravery, the tide of the Revolution soon turned in the South. My husband and I recognized that Southerners possessed that same roughness as the Scottish citizen.

Castles in the Snow

Scottish emigration to the colonies soared to 145,000 between 1707 and 1775. The Scots had better incentives to emigrate due to poorer conditions. When England and Scotland joined in 1707, forming the United Kingdom, they received access to all of the colonies. This perk was another reason for the increase in migration.

The Scottish Diaspora was in three separate streams: Lowland Scots, Highland Scots, and Ulster-Scots. The Ulster-Scots commonly were referred to as Scots-Irish. Many people refer to them as Irish-Scot, but that is not correct. The correct reference is Scots-Irish. In the 1740s, the upcoming French and Indian War (1754-1763) caused more frequent Indian raids along the Pennsylvania frontier. Many Scots-Irish took to the Great Wagon Road from there to the states of both North and South Carolina.

The Scots-Irish were mainly Protestant, while most of the Irish in the Carolinas were Catholic. The significant influx of Scots-Irish into South Carolina began in the late 1730s. By 1790, the US Census indicated almost 32.9% Scots and 11.7% Irish living in that state. Today, the sense of connection between the two areas remains inside Charleston.

Thomas found the correlation significant, and he persuaded me with such facts to make a move. I agreed that there was more than a kindred spirit between the two areas; there was even more than a bond of ancestry. What seemed to exist was a deep and abiding love and respect for each other. All of these facts allowed me peace to leave my family, friends, and even my country for a place that I had never seen. Although our ending wasn't what I hoped, my love for Scotland will always remain.

Chapter Two

I remained uncomfortable while the fire continued to blaze in the room. Whoever built that inferno meant to protect me, but from what? *Where is Thomas? Am I dying?* I remembered reading that just before someone passed, their life flashed before their eyes. Without warning, vivid memories, hiding in the recesses of my mind, rolled out in perfect detail. Is it reasonable to remember events from five years of age?

My first memory of Thomas Baxter Reid flooded my mind in vivid part. It was a blustery cold day inside The Battery of Charleston, South Carolina. At the age of five, I had pirouetted in my perfect form, at least perfect to me, in front of my window. The moving trucks had finally departed after depositing our treasures inside the new home, which seemed like a castle. I noticed a handsome young boy around my age looking at my house. He stood in the back driveway, staring up as if he could see me.

I now giggled like a five-year-old as I vividly recalled that day. My vain attempt to wave at him now, tonight, was thwarted by my inability to move my hands.

Maybe, briefly, I had become that little child from long ago. Anything remained possible in this night of suspended time. It felt incredulous to laugh while in my situation. Most people might have experienced terror or panic, but I didn't. Instead, I laughed at old memories. *Maybe, I've injured my brain?*

Although the young boy from long ago stared, it was impossible that he could see me unless he had an extraordinary vision that could penetrate the antique windows and shutters. Shamelessly, I watched this handsome creature with shining blond hair and large chocolate-colored eyes. A powerful sense told me that the boy who stood before me would be a major player in my life.

Momma's image now followed that of my husband as I recalled being homeschooled by her. Without a doubt, my momma was the most beautiful woman in the world. Long blond hair cascaded around the face of an angel. Like me, she was small, with a smile that would soften the hearts of all she met. Her eyes were deep brown and shone outward from the fairest skin, also like mine. When she walked, her steps were like the glide of an angel. Lightly, she trod this earth. Her voice was soft, almost musical when she cuddled me at night. I was an only child. Oh, how I miss her.

My being an only child pleased me because of all the drama next door at the Reid house. The two boys there, Maxwell and Thomas, constantly competed in everything. Once Thom and I proclaimed our desire to wed, at the age of five, Max hounded me with taunts and silly insults. I preferred my peaceful home to their constant drama. People could say what they liked about large families, but mine felt perfect to me.

That memory faded as another one played faster than I ever dreamed. Upon graduation from college, my new husband and I had settled into our small historic cottage located only blocks from the wedding-cake house where I was born and the golden home of the Reid family inside The Battery of Charleston. The new home that Thom and I purchased was brick that we painted a shining white; it was reminiscent of the earlier home, the wedding-cake house that I had loved.

Mrs. Reid had shocked the neighborhood when she painted their tired old red brick a flaming gold many years earlier. In the evenings, it beckoned because the gold appeared to be solid 24 karats. Behind it lay a brand-new infinity swimming pool where we spent most of our young lives. Did secrets we whispered into those stifling, honeysuckle nights remain suspended in the air?

Years earlier, my husband and I had agreed not to have children. That was fine with me. My deep love for him and writing surely would be enough. My books became my children while I loved each one. They had become popular, at least around Charleston, while my husband's reputation as an architect blossomed. Life was good until Momma died suddenly. To this day, I will forever hear Josey, our beloved family maid, calmly tell me that Momma "was gone." I wondered why Josey would call to alert me that Momma had gone somewhere.

"Well, where did she go?" I asked. At that moment, Thomas burst into our house. Charleston wasn't that small, with a population of 802,122 residents. Nevertheless, as in most southern towns, the locals were very tight, so word reached him at about the same time that I heard the news.

My attachment to Josey was that of a child to a mother. I loved her just as much. She was the one who dried my tears and put the

Band-Aids on my knees. If I wanted answers, she seemed more attuned to what I needed—more than Momma.

Lovingly, I recalled how I found out about my unknown uncle, that scoundrel Robert Corbett. Whenever I thought of him, the ugly face of Edward Teach (Blackbeard), who was a greedy, bloodthirsty man, came to the forefront of my mind. I supposed Momma and Daddy thought I didn't need to know about my unknown relative, but Josey believed I did. That evening, when I trod down the stairs to her small apartment, at the foot of them, I hesitated before I knocked on the door. Even though Josey often brought me here, Momma insisted that I must never knock at her door. It was okay if Josey took me there, but I must never bother her. I had only done this once before. Momma always stressed this was Josey's "little house," which was her "off" time, so we shouldn't be a nuisance. I knew my friend wouldn't mind, no matter what Momma said.

Gently, I knocked, but there was no response. It was late. Softly, I opened the door. The gentle snores which greeted me made me smile. Our beloved maid refused to cut back on her work, and I realized she must be tired.

"Josey, Josey!" I whispered into the perfumed air of her simple rooms. The flowers that she took from Mrs. Reid's trash next door looked fresh to me. I waited.

"Miss Caroline? That you, honey?" Poor Josey, her silver hair stood up on end as she slowly moved toward me. She looked like a ghost. Still, I waited. If Daddy or Momma found us, there would be more drama. I couldn't take much more of the whispers around our wedding-cake house. Something was up, and I would find the truth here, tonight, from Josey.

"Josey, yes, it's me. You know why I'm here. Tell me who Robert is." I stood on the threshold, waiting for her to invite me inside.

Josey motioned with her right hand that I could enter. "Where'd you hear that name? I don't know of a Robert." I knew she was avoiding the subject because she wouldn't look at me, and her gaze continuously darted around my presence.

"Now, you see here, Josephine. If my mother knows him, so do you. So, fess up! I'm not leaving until you talk."

Josey looked relieved. I knew she wanted to tell me but not without being forced. I had just compelled her. She moved deliberately like maybe her hip hurt. She rubbed the right one as she walked. I never saw her do that, but this was her private space. There was no pretense here.

She motioned for me to sit at her four-chair little chrome table. Mom had insisted over and over that we replace it, but the old thing was from her past. She loved it and refused Momma's offer for a new and better set. The chairs had red plastic backs and seats. One contained a significant split; I sat there. Automatically, she began to make hot chocolate with a "ton of cream." I smiled. My friend was such a nurturer.

"If I's tell you this, I's putting myself in a bad place. Your parents won't take kindly to me meddling in family affairs." She kept looking at the door like she was expecting them to break into the room. Again, I waited. I knew that if I pushed too hard, she would clam up and never explain things.

Wearily, she lowered herself into the chair beside me with her own cup of cocoa, sans the cream. She was looking far away when she began the story that changed my life, like in a trance. No one could tell a story like Josey. On many evenings when Momma and Daddy left me with her, Josey would tell scary tales that would keep me awake for several nights. I never told my parents. I feared that they might stop her. Josey was quite the drama queen.

"Let me begin by telling you again that if your momma or daddy ever hears that I's told you their business, well, I's be in trouble for sure. Miss Caroline, I's just not comfortable doing this." She moved to stand but instead lowered her eyes.

I did understand that I placed her in an uncomfortable position, but what would my parents do to her? Fire her? Never, because since I could remember, there was Josey.

Josephine Nellie Hendricks was a part of our family. Her ancestors were forced to flee Charleston in 1670. They were slaves brought from the English colony of Barbados. The family worked for a group of wealthy planters who owned acreage in Charleston's surrounding area. The home they occupied was destroyed in a fire centuries earlier, but the family remained tied to Charleston's history. Antiquity filled my beloved Charleston with good and evil, as everywhere else must attest. Beloved Josey had seldom referenced those days that faded into her past. I guessed it was so painful. It was now too late for me to ask her to share her memories. It would have probably pleased her if I had shown interest in her life events, but I never had time for such things back then. Yes, Charleston held demons hidden in her past.

"Aye, and Scotland, you are not free from your times of forced captivity!" Shouting the words in my overheated room, inside Alladale, I shook my head. *I'm becoming terribly confused.* I considered that the heat might have cooked my brain.

So many thoughts overtook me. They jumped from one to another in my muddled mind as it searched…for what? Panic filled me. An urgent feeling that I must remember each word Thom had ever uttered. Moving at lightning speed, bits and pieces of his life were delivered. I saw his face hovering before me. He appeared angry, as if I wasn't paying proper attention to his instructions, which began as whispers but quickly escalated to shouts.

"Throughout history, there were reports of both the Scottish and Welsh who took captives as slaves during their raids. Such action appeared to cease in the thirteenth century. See Scotland; you also have a history of slaves. Just look at what you have done to my wife!" Hearing those words in my mind made me realize that I, too, was a slave. Not like Josey but in a different way; I, also, was bound and had been stripped of my freedom.

"Thomas, you are angry at me. What have I done?" He continued to hover over me as a vision.

Suddenly, I recalled sitting with Thomas on many evenings in Charleston while watching the adults outside the large windows of his golden house, surrounded by the darkness. We whispered stories of slaves, ghosts, and pirates. I now realized that there existed a history of all of them both inside Charleston and Scotland; legends fanned our fears. Josey had fueled our love for these obsessions.

With the thought of ghosts, I now witnessed Paula Prissy Peterson's face. That beautiful face woke me from a deep sleep. I hated to be forced from the gentle arms of respite to deal with this overheated room of doom. My entire body was drenched with sweat, even though the room was now quite chilly. *Will her spirit never leave me? Why do I see HER face? Is she coming for me?* I passed out, either from fear or weariness. I was transported to the sixth-grade dance, the time when I learned the meaning of death. I cried out, "Please, don't make me remember this. Haven't I suffered enough? What have I done? Please, help me! Go away, Paula. I've paid for my meanness to you."

When the new kid had first moved to our slice of heaven inside of Charleston, I didn't like her. She competed with me for the love of my Thomas. Already, at the age of five, I loved him. I also treasured his brother Max. The Reid boys passed me from one to the other through the years. Never did it enter my mind to find a new boyfriend. There was no one else. I had named Paula, "Prissy Peterson," in my attempt to turn Thom from her.

"Caroline, turn one more time toward Max! That's it, honey; you guys look so great. Paula, take Thom's hand, yes, that's the way, sweetie, beautiful! Okay, let's get one more."

Daddy and Momma had gone crazy. Dad had produced a large camera that he never used until this special night. Later in the evening, we would be grateful for the photos of a beloved person happily laughing before a tragic death.

"Daddy, you have like a gazillion photos. That's enough!" Daddy laughed with glee.

I had to admit that the four of us had shone on that special evening. By this time, I had made peace with Paula. I realized that I couldn't change Thom's infatuation with the lovely blond girl. Max was my boyfriend at the time; the Reid boys had once again switched me as they did until they found someone better. One of them always came back to me.

Max looked like a polished copper penny on that fateful evening while his blond-haired brother glowed. Paula's cobalt-blue dress gleamed like sapphires. My burgundy dress reminded me of a glass of Momma's claret, which she now enjoyed.

Finally, Daddy stepped back with his camera. Alex, the Peterson's driver, had stood quietly by the front door, during this period of family memories, while my parents and those of Max and Thom gabbed away. The Petersons weren't able to see us off because Mrs. Peterson, Emily, was hosting a significant gala at her art gallery. Paula's family was seldom in town. Most of the time, Paula stayed with her nanny, Gloria.

Alex appeared eager to get us moving. "Sir, we should get the young people loaded into the car. We have to drive across town for the other two." He nodded and smiled at our little group.

I could tell that Daddy didn't want us to leave. *Did he have a feeling, as I did, that something ominous was about to occur?* Slowly, he walked with us to the door as the others continued to laugh. Mom and Mrs. Reid were enjoying another glass of claret as our dad's sipped beers. Life was good. They seemed proud of us. *How could we know what waited?*

Daddy opened the door. He frowned. "Oh, no, it's raining. The meteorologists have it wrong yet again. Let me get some umbrellas. Now, Alex, you be sure and bring this beauty back to me." He waved a giant black parasol, with white engravings that glowed on the handle toward the young driver who nodded with a grin. Poor Alex, his life was about to be destroyed. After this night, I would never see him again.

I felt Max's hand on my right arm as we stepped down the wet steps. I turned, and I'll never forget seeing Thom and Paula teetering on the top level. They appeared happy as Thomas clasped her hand, just as in an earlier childhood dream, their fingers clenched so tightly. We were all laughing and gay; this night was the first big event in our young lives. There was no stopping us!

Gaily, we huddled in the back seat of the Bentley. Recently, the Petersons traded in their Bentley sedan for a Bentayga, which had seven seats. It was dark blue and gray like the other one had been, which matched the color of their pristine house. Everything about this new family seemed perfect.

Slowly, Alex backed out of our drive and headed across town to pick up Lyle and Shelly. They were friends of the others at their private school. I had never gone to school because I was homeschooled and was nervous about going to a real one. That was the disadvantage of homeschooling—I had become a bit of a loner. Whenever I thought about attending a public gathering, I became anxious.

Unending laughter filled the car, almost drowning out the sound of the torrential downpour. The wind blew the rain in sheets as pieces of shrubs and small trees hit the vehicle. Daddy was correct: they sure called it wrong tonight. I knew that if my daddy had known about this monsoon, he would have insisted that our chauffeur, Bryan, drive us. Not because of anything against Alex, but that was my daddy.

I seldom ventured into this part of town. My world existed in The Battery and a few surrounding streets. There was nothing for me in this area. It wasn't that I was a snob, but I had no friends here or any other reason to come into this place. Becoming aware of the driving rain, we soon quieted. The arrangement was that we would drive to Shelly's house. This kid, Lydell, her date, would be waiting for us there with Shelly. When we pulled up to the small house, I realized that I knew nothing of this girl's world. Everyone I knew had chauffeurs and lived in mansions. It wasn't necessary, but I realized there was another world out there that I had never experienced. Shelly's little cottage appeared sad and unkempt.

We remained quiet as Alex carried Daddy's umbrella to the small house. I could see his big smile as he waited while getting pelted by the storm. He was a great guy. I supposed it was Mrs. Thorpe who opened the door. Her rose dress looked pretty. The white apron suggested that she must be cooking. I would come to know that Shelly's mom looked like an older version of her daughter with long blond hair that swept off her face. She was lovely. Mrs. Thorpe waved to us with a worried look as she gazed up into the heavens. For a brief moment, she hesitated. Then Shelly's mom glanced at us again. We all waved back but realized that she probably couldn't see us.

Alex remained standing in the rain as he courteously awaited the others. In a matter of minutes, the two kids barreled toward us. There were no photo sessions from this little family, or maybe they were finished. I could hear Lydell teasing Alex about something.

The chauffeur sheltered them from the rain; Daddy's umbrella was getting quite a workout. When the two young people climbed into the car, I'll never forget their faces. Shelly's hair looked stunning in an up-do, much like Paula's and mine. Her soft yellow dress suited her, and Lydell took my breath away in his white blazer and dark blue slacks. It was funny that all three girls wore almost the same style of dress but in different colors. Both of the guys wore white jackets and dark slacks, except Max, who insisted on wearing some retro-hipster suit of orange and green. Only he could have pulled it off without looking tacky.

The new Bentley was rated as the top luxury car in the world. We breathed deeply of that luxurious new-car smell. All of us knew how blessed we were. As we approached the academy, Alex completely halted at a stop sign. When he began to move ahead, out of nowhere, quickly, a speeding vehicle plowed into the right side of the car. I remembered hearing him shout. The hit jarred us, and the noise of the impact was impossibly loud. There were no sounds from us. Immediately, Alex slammed on the brakes. We all jerked forward then were slapped backward into our seats.

Paula moved differently. Maybe she was trying to turn to look at the four of us behind her. I'm not sure, but I was watching as her head smacked into the side window. It made a sickening sound. We all assured Alex that we were okay so that he could move the vehicle across the street into the academy's drive. Although we were dazed and shaking, it appeared we had all survived without harm.

Our driver sustained a bloody nose and clutched a handkerchief to it. Such a hard rain caused the blood to dilute when it ran in a little stream from his nose. I noticed that he was shaking all over. A crowd assembled in the rain. The headmaster ran toward us. I saw that he didn't carry an umbrella. I wanted to remind Alex to share Daddy's with him. When Dr. Bauer, the headmaster, opened Paula's door, she fell out onto the wet pavement. I heard his cry. The rest is a blur.

Everyone was yelling, and Alex fell to the ground beside Paula with loud sobs. Thomas ran to the limp girl in hysterics, picked her up from the wet tarmac, and gently hugged her. His screams pierced the air. For several minutes, that's all I heard. Rain poured from his blond hair, and his face glistened with it. The headmaster cradled the two soaked young people in his arms. There wasn't any blood from Paula, so I briefly wondered if she was joking. Seeing her lying on the pathway in that deluge, dressed in her gorgeous cobalt-blue dress, will always be a part of my psyche. Long strands of her beautiful blond hair hung in drenched sheets around her small angelic face.

Life stood still. Maybe Thomas never recovered from the loss of his first love. We referenced her for the remainder of our lives.

Even today, I experience trouble trying to recall the sequence of events. I remembered entering the school. The festive decorations and lights appeared silly. Beautiful dresses were bedraggled and stunning hairstyles now fell around wet, pale faces. They put Thom in an ambulance because he wouldn't stop screaming. My body was shaking so severely that I couldn't breathe; my teeth clattered as someone put Max and me inside a stranger's car. There was no new-car smell. When we reached the hospital, our parents waited for us. Dr. Lafferty, our pediatrician, rushed to me with a big hug. I buried my face against his starched shirt and wished Josey was also there.

Thom spent the night in the hospital, highly sedated. Max and I were driven home by my daddy, who refused to allow our chauffeur to drive. The Reid family rode home with us; there was no sound but the incessant noise of rain and wind. Paula Quinn Peterson's death was my first experience with the Grim Reaper.

"I know you're coming for me! Why are you waiting? Please, come and get me. How much longer do I have to suffer?" My words were a murmur before I returned to that time long ago and the red dinette set. Paula's death was an essential link in our story.

Chapter Three

I shuffled through the neurons inside my brain, finally arriving back at the red dinette set inside Josey's little apartment at the foot of the stairs in Charleston's wedding-cake house.

Honestly, I knew this wasn't fair to her, but I quietly watched as she once again set two large cups of hot chocolate on the table. My cup filled with freshly whipped cream, just the way I liked it. I wondered how Josey always seemed to have whatever I needed. I loved the smell of flowers and chocolate that filled her space. As she tended a wound or my broken spirit, she always presented me with the best cup of cocoa in the world, which contained a generous dollop of real cream. Quickly, I grabbed it and felt the sweet, soothing liquid slip down the back of my throat. I knew from the look in her eyes that I would be changed when I left here. Not saying a word, I lowered my eyes and patiently waited.

"Miss Caroline, you have an uncle named Robert James Corbett. You know that there is great wealth in your family?" She stared into my eyes.

What is she about to reveal? Were my ancestors' slave traders or pirates? I simply nodded agreement. Never had I witnessed Josey as somber as she appeared to seek the right words. When she weaved magical stories of ghosts, her words came easily. *Why is this so difficult?*

"Well, your Momma's childhood and that of Mr. Robert was happy. I worked for your grandmama when I was a youngster. Did ya know that?"

I shook my head. There was so much that I didn't know about her. Josey was a very private person. My being a child prevented any interest in her life. Instead, I talked only of myself. Now I wished to speak with her again. There were many questions to ask.

"Well, she was a fine lady—the finest I ever knowed, except for your momma. Your family, they's noble and proud, they's history is hard work and great success. Those ancestors, whose blood flows in you, was smart and well-respected. Your momma was one of Charleston's debutantes, just like you gonna be. Now, this is something to be proud of, no matter what folks today may say. You can't change history, and you can't hide success.

"I want you to go to that ball. Your momma says you don't want to attend. I can tell you that Miss Elizabeth Eisenhour's family will force her to go; I's excellent friends with Missy Bollock, their maid." Josey took a long swallow of the sweet chocolate. Then, she studied me for a moment.

Elizabeth was Max's girlfriend at that time long ago. Our presentation was in December, but I hesitated. *Is this happening? Did Josey just encourage me to attend the Cotillion?* I knew she usually thought such things were trivial. *Yes, it feels a little silly, but now I won't miss it.*

"Well, the thing is, your momma was engaged to Mr. Robert's best friend, Mr. Jack. Those two men attended the Citadel together. They was like brothers; I's heard. The wedding date waited. I think I heard that Miss Kayce had purchased the most beautiful gown in the world. She was excited. Anyway, about two months before the big day, your momma met your daddy, Mark. It was love at first sight. She confided in me late one evening, right here in this room." I glanced around the room as though hoping to see Momma.

"She sat right there. Where you's sittin' now when she told me that she couldn't marry the fine young cadet because Mr. Mark stole her heart. Now, your daddy is another fine person. He's a hard worker. That hardware store has been here about as long as this city. Haven't you ever wondered how you live such a fine life? Have you never questioned how a hardware store could provide mansions and chauffeurs and a staff of people to wait on you?"

I felt rather stupid as I shook my head. Never had I considered such things because finances didn't interest me. My heart dwelled in the fine arts. Suddenly, I wondered how Daddy could afford all of this.

"Well, he can't. Don't get me wrong. He makes a good living, but he could never afford all of this." She waved her hand around the room as if my wedding-cake house was a castle, and it was to me. Her tale was becoming so interesting that I leaned almost into Josey's lap.

"Mr. Robert threatened your momma. He had a conniption at the betrayal of his friend. At about that time, your grandparents died in the boating accident out there on the Colonial Lake. Before their untimely deaths, they had established a hefty trust fund for their two children. Honey, when I's says hefty, I's means it! That scoundrel, Mr. Robert, he took your momma to court. That cuss demanded that she be disinherited. It seemed ridiculous, but her brother connived with a judge friend who was also a friend with that ol' Mr. Jack. They tied up things in court for years and years. Many a person would have stopped trying, but your parents' attorney took him on in all the courts.

"In the meantime, your momma and daddy married. Your folks enjoyed their happy lives. It didn't appear to harm them, at least not in the beginning. When you turned the age of four, the matter settled, and your momma got her fair inheritance. They immediately purchased this house and began to renovate it. One year later, we all moved here.

"Well, that's your history, and it seems a shame that nobody 'cept me told you. Caroline, you's has an uncle named Robert Corbett out there. Your grandparents, God rest their souls; they would cas in their graves."

I wasn't sure what "cas" meant but felt certain it wasn't good. I pictured my grandmama and grandpapa looking at each other in their dark tomb. My world changed. My life was not as it earlier had seemed. Many might have felt angry for not having been told of an uncle, but not me. Instead, I felt pride in my mother and father—what a love story! Briefly, I thought of Thom. *Will our family and friends someday hear a story about such courage and devotion between us?* I could only hope.

Josey had appeared drawn. Often, I thought about what we might do as she aged. No one could ever replace her. *I must suggest to Momma that we give her more time to herself.* She looked ancient, yet she was the first to get up in the morning and the only one to set a formal breakfast buffet on our antique sideboard. Everything she did was flawless.

My trusted friend had just betrayed the confidence of my parents by sharing this story with me. I would never forget such an act of love. My head was filled with wondering how I might get the truth out of my parents without endangering Josey. I now felt a need in my heart to discuss this with my family. Gently, I kissed her sweet cheek.

"You get some sleep, Josey. Why don't you sleep late tomorrow? Daddy seldom eats breakfast. Half the time, Momma doesn't get up before ten. Please? You just sleep late."

A faint smile greeted my words; maybe she briefly considered my offer. She stared into my eyes, and I looked deeply into her big brown ones, which had seen more pain than I could ever imagine. Then she shook her head.

"Miss Caroline, you go on now. I's can't sleep late even if I's wanted. My's old body wouldn't let me." Gently, she chuckled as she shook her head and waved her right hand in the air.

I went to the door and turned one more time. I hoped that I would never forget this moment and the love of a true friend. When I opened the door, there stood Daddy with his arms crossed over his chest. He did not look happy. I heard a small gasp from Josey.

"You go upstairs, right now, Caroline! I need to have a word with her." He pointed at Josey, who bowed her head.

Daddy's bark was more significant than his bite. We considered Josey a member of our family. All of us loved her so much. Later, Josey chuckled when she told me that Daddy had apologized to her for not telling me about my uncle. This discovery freed me to discuss old Uncle Robert with my parents, but I never did.

Chapter Four

Upon my mother's death, my beloved Josey had again rushed to my side. She offered me support and dried my tears. Once my dear friend entered our home, I didn't have to be concerned with making decisions. Silently, she came, and she cared for Thomas and me. Having her at my side reminded me of my idyllic childhood and the security she always provided.

Daddy requested that we plan a funeral, but Momma often said she never wanted such a horrendous thing, with people filing past her rose-colored casket, commenting on how beautiful she looked, especially ol' Sissy Smothers. Momma remarked that she had never seen a dead person look beautiful.

"If I'm not pretty enough for you in life, don't ya be thinkin' I might look better when I'm dead!" I heard Josey's words in there.

I doubted that ol' Sissy even existed for the longest time, but then I found out she was about a hundred years old and loved funerals. *Well, she would be disappointed with the death of this Charlestonian.* Josey had stood up to Daddy and reinforced my words.

"Momma doesn't want a funeral. Sissy Smothers will have to wait for someone else to die." Josey winked at me.

Yes, Josey was always my champion. And here she came once again, rushing to my side on the death of my beloved Momma. At that time, my friend lived with me for about three weeks until she felt sure that I had appropriately begun to grieve. Thomas loved her as much as I did. In fact, we begged her to move to Scotland with us. But Josey wouldn't leave Daddy. Once, right before we departed, she told me that she would have gone with us if Momma hadn't died, but I doubted that. As much as I knew she loved me, she loved Momma and Daddy more.

Not long after we buried Momma, her creepy brother, Robert (alias Blackbeard), began to harass our family once more. *How much money does he need?* Earlier, his actions hurt Momma. He still hated my daddy because of the Jack incident. The word was that Momma humiliated ol' Jack when she left him crying at the altar. Neither Jack nor Uncle Robert ever recovered from her betrayal. Before Momma was planted in the ground, that scoundrel filed another lawsuit against us.

He claimed that we shouldn't receive what remained of Momma's hefty trust fund from my grandparents. It was ridiculous, but, once again, he dragged our name through the dirt. It almost destroyed my daddy and tarnished Thom's sterling reputation as a new architect. I didn't understand how much my husband suffered over this until we left Charleston. Eventually, the case was thrown out of court, but the damage was done. All of this only enforced Thom's desire to leave Charleston for Inverness, Scotland.

My eyes popped opened when I completed this memory/dream. "What a blessed life I've received. I never realized all that my parents did to shelter me."

My family had always shown great love and respect for each other and all those around them. I questioned, *Who would do such an unthinkable thing to me?* "If only I can remember the moments leading up to this!" I strained to pull at that particular thread of memory, but I failed.

Instead, as if in comfort mode, my thoughts rushed to Scotland, my adopted home. I loved Her immediately, from the often-turbulent waters of the coast to the blessed Highlands. Her history was splendid, with all sorts of exciting events, just like my beloved Charleston. Both held tales of pirates and warriors. Was there ever any braver than those Scots who fought at the Battle of Culloden? That controversial battle happened on April 16, 1846, marking the end of the Jacobite uprising with a substantial, decisive government victory.

Just as divisive was the beginning of the American Civil War, which started when the secessionist forces attacked Fort Sumter, located in Charleston, South Carolina; that battle happened on April 12, 1861. Plus, Scotland also suffered her own civil war between the Bruce dynasty and long-term rivals, Comyn-Balliol. It lasted until the middle of the fourteenth century. This willingness to fight to the grave was an example of the similarity between the two places I had grown to love.

I heard Thomas's voice coming from above me, loudly explaining this to me once again. "Do ya not see the similarities? Ya must see it, April 16 and April 12, and only fifteen years difference. Both of these lands flowed with the blood of the brave who fought to the death for what they believed! Maybe today, we realize it was not the right thing, but there's a pattern to these two places we love!" His brown eyes held a fire that couldn't be erased when he looked at me, now, in my head. "Aye, Caroline, now ye must fight! Ye fight 'til the end. Do ya hear me?"

"Aye, I do, and I'll fight, but I'm tired," I wondered how I was to battle with my hands shackled, but it felt important that I acknowledge his words. "My battle's not clear to me. I'm dying for both places that I love. Is that what you want me to understand?"

I felt an urgency to understand Charleston's likeness, with her steamy summers and coastal breezes, and Scotland, with her west coast bordered by the Atlantic Ocean and her east by the North Sea. South Carolina had a dramatically different summer and winter. Scotland's temperatures remained temperate because it was warmed by the Gulf Stream of the Atlantic Ocean.

"But this is a difference, not the same." I wanted to point out this variance to him. He continued to hover over my bed.

Thomas became angry. "Look for the link, Caroline. That same Gulf Stream of the Atlantic also flows only fifty miles from Charleston. If you are to survive, you must think! Be smarter than whoever is doing this to you."

"Yes, I understand. I'll try harder and do better."

"Aye, now yer beginning to see. Don't you know that Scotland's west side is warmer than her east thanks to the influence of the mighty Atlantic Ocean's currents, which combine with the North Sea's cooling effect? Do ya see another connection those currents can have? Think of the hurricane season. It exists in both Scotland and Charleston. Although the latter has more than her fair share."

I nodded as if he watched me. *Is it really him? If so, how can he remain suspended in the air over my bed?*

His voice continued to boom with facts. "Scotland was raided by the Vikings, who arrived in the eighth century. They searched for slaves and luxury items. Charleston was frequently looted by many pirates, including Blackbeard, Stede Bonnet, Charles Vane, and Anne Bonny, who hailed from Charleston. They captured innocent people and carried them away as slaves." Yes, the two places couldn't be more different, but alike.

None of this made sense to me, so for a long time, I lay motionless. My mind burned with much fleeting information. All of it appeared trivial.

"Thom, what should I do with these facts? Will something in them help me?" There was no answer, just more facts arriving quicker than I could digest them.

"When Irish settlers moved to Scotland, they brought the Gaelic language." I recalled how quickly Thomas mastered it, but I had struggled. A faint smile briskly tugged at my lips but couldn't remain. My fear and discomfort had stripped me of the luxury of a grin. Plus, my brain worked in high gear, trying to decipher all of the random information.

The thought occurred to me that I just might be crazy. Not only had I lost all control of my extremities, but my mind raged.

"During the nineteenth century, Glasgow became one of the largest cities in the world. It was known as 'the second city of the empire' after London. Also, during this time, a process of rehabilitation for the Highlands occurred. In the 1820s, during the Romantic Revival, the tartan and kilt were adopted by the social elite, not only in Scotland but across Europe. Today, in the United

States, many proud descendants of Scotland sported kilts." Thomas continued to hang over me as he spouted Scottish facts.

"Aye, Thom, and you were one of them." I nodded at his face, which also seemed unable to smile.

"The Highlands remained impoverished during the 1800s; they experienced frequent periods of famine. It was the only part of mainland Britain to do so. However, at the end of the nineteenth century, Scotland's population continued to grow despite many hardships. Just as Charleston was left tattered, with families starving after the Civil War, they also had fought to recover. Many never attained their earlier wealth, but the South once again prospered and grew." The words stopped briefly.

Although my husband had never served in the military, both of our fathers had. All of us were proud of Scotland's important part in the British efforts of the First World War. Thomas referred to their bravery so often; they provided manpower, ships, machinery, fish, and money. "Alba," an old name for Scotland, sent over a half million men to the war. Over a quarter of those died in combat, many from disease, and 150,000 were seriously wounded. He frequently said, "Ya shouldn't mess with a man dressed in a skirt. Aye, they're mean."

The thought of war made me consider that during the Second World War, Nazi Germany targeted Scotland because of its shipbuilding, coal mines, and factories. German bombers hit Glasgow and Edinburgh. The most significant air raid that occurred there, the Clydebank Blitz, took place in 1941. The Germans hoped to destroy shipbuilding in the area. Five hundred twenty-eight people were killed, and four thousand homes were destroyed.

I recalled that Charleston proudly held the Naval Shipyard, a US Navy shipbuilding and repair facility located along the west bank of the Cooper River in North Charleston.

"Aye, Thomas, you shouldn't get angry. I get it! Once again, I followed the link, but what does this accomplish?"

My answer was more facts continuing to bombard my ears. "The locals in Scotland still talked about the time that Rudolf Hess flew to Renfrewshire with the hopes of brokering peace through the Duke of Hamilton. When Hitler received the letter in which Hess described his actions, Hitler remarked that it was one of the worst betrayals of his life. He considered it a personal insult."

Yes, Scotland held a rich and varied past, as did Charleston. Once again, my mind returned to one of the worst periods of US history. The American Civil War had pitted brother against brother, father against son. The soldiers from Charleston were as brave as any and fiercely fought for what they believed, just as the Scots had done in their time of struggle.

At one time, Scotland was home to the brown bear, lynx, elk, walrus, and, of course, Thom's favorite, the wolf. They were hunted to extinction in historic times. Thank God our golden eagle still flew. It remained an icon, and it was hailed as our Scottish national bird. Often, Thom and I witnessed the majesty of such a large predator soaring in the blue skies over our beloved Alladale located in the Highlands. Inverness had a population of 48,201 people, which made it the twelfth largest city in Scotland.

Charleston's number of residents ranked it as the largest city in South Carolina, with 133,762 folks.

My mind continued to jump with facts. Some related, others different. What I wanted was to remember every word my husband had ever spoken in my presence. I believed that when my brain stopped delivering information it considered vital, I would die. I fought to pull facts from the past: our blue and white flag boldly displayed the saltire associated with St. Andrew. He was martyred bound to an X-shaped cross.

Thomas used to sigh and say that the thistle was the country's floral emblem. "Aye, only Scotland would choose the thistle." Yet, he stressed that not all thistles were considered weeds. "There are several species that are non-invasive but are well-behaved and benefit the health of our working lands and natural areas."

I heard him sing "The Flower of Scotland." With a faraway look, he recited that the thistle became the emblem of Scotland during the reign of Alexander III.

Why won't his face leave me? He continues to hover over me! I have lost my mind?

Legend whispered that an army of King Haakon of Norway, intent upon conquering the Scots on the coast of Lars in the deep of night, had planned to surprise the sleeping Scottish clansmen. In their attempt at surprise, they removed their shoes. Unfortunately, one of his men stepped on a thistle. The scream which filled the night air awakened the clansmen—and they won the battle.

"Sort of like ye, Caroline. Ya little, but ya make me scream with passion, ya know?" I did understand because he created the same feeling in me. My heart longed to see him again, in person, not just hovering over me like this spirit, which wouldn't leave.

All of this and so much more, I learned from a man who would give the shirt off his back and fight to the death for those he loved. With that thought, I could no longer keep the tears from flowing. My mind and body were tired of the battle. *Perhaps my husband is correct, and I should fight.* Instead, I cried until my eyes felt swollen. Mucus and tears dripped down my cheeks, but I was unable to wipe them away. Instead, they dried on my face. The crusty sensation resulted in a feeling of tightness around my eyes.

What does any of it matter? I lie in a cold bed with no food or water. Whoever built this fire of protection must have met a tragic end. Was it Thomas?

"Aye, what more will ya be forced to endure before yer death?" My whisper hung in the hot air of the silent room.

Chapter Five

While I waited to die, all remained as well as possible because of the trusty fire that became my only friend during this torment. "Friend?" That word carried me back to Charleston in my brain's attempt to maintain what little sanity that remained. The fire had begun to wane slightly, which frightened me. Although the room felt much better with less heat, I feared the result as the temperature continued to plunge. *What conditions wait for me later in the night?* I considered it would be a blessing if I didn't wake.

Now even the room changed from comforting to eerie. Strange noises carried on the night air, weird, crying sounds that I had never before heard. *So, is this my first evening shackled in my torture chamber?* Several times, I tried to slide lower under the covers for protection but couldn't because of the restraints. *How long will the frightening sounds continue? And when will the effects of dehydration begin?* I desperately had to use the toilet but tried to hold it as long as I could. My bladder felt ready to burst, but, for now, I would maintain my human dignity as long as I could. *When I lose that, I will lose myself.* I dreaded the thought of losing my pride before death took me.

I spied the antique cupboard at the back of the room. A soft lilac blanket waited on the top shelf. I longed to walk over and bring it to the bed. The luxurious feel of the soft cashmere would make me happy. My throat was parched, and I could barely speak, but I whispered my stark reality. "No one cares if you are happy."

My mind took me to a place that was the beginning of an essential time in my past. Eventually, this also involved the death of Paula Peterson. *Maybe these morose thoughts continue because your end is drawing ever closer?* There appeared to be no sequence or pattern to the invasion of my mind.

Once more, I went to my childhood to reminisce. Before my third-grade school year began, a new girl moved into the house, two doors from the Reid boys and me. We heard a year earlier that the property had sold and watched each day for the moving van. Hopefully, a cool kid would arrive and fit nicely into our little group. Instead, all we saw for over a year were workers and big trucks, which decimated the previously gorgeous yard. We grew weary of the noise and the ugly site.

Finally, a week before my homeschool classes began, a local landscape company, Greene's, showed up with truckloads of dark, fertile soil, sod, gorgeous trees, and shrubs. Thom called to report that he and Max and their mother were sitting on the front porch watching the show. His mother was a fanatic about lawns and shrubs. My momma couldn't care less about gardening but allowed me to join them.

What transpired was indeed a miracle. An ugly gash of disturbed soil in our pristine neighborhood had become a glowing green gem by evening. All-day, we sat there mesmerized by the process. Mrs. Reid knew every plant as well as the type of grass, which I tried to remember. *Zoysia, that is it.* Lovingly, the landscapers planted each plant in the perfect place, at least according to Mrs. Reid.

My eyes opened only to discover that, unfortunately, my own surroundings hadn't changed. A small groan escaped me. "Okay, you have a plan. Keep remembering pleasant memories. Recall all those who love you and whom you love. Don't allow yourself to panic! You are loved, you are loved." Over and over, I repeated that phrase as if it might save me. I felt like Dorothy in The Wizard of Oz when she repeatedly whispered, "There's no place like home!"

My thoughts always returned to those I loved the most, and my husband, Thomas Baxter Reid, was at the forefront. Once again, his image flashed before me. He stood on a hilltop dressed in his beloved kilt, his dark eyes staring into the distance.

"Aye, what do ya see, Thomas? What's happened to us? I know it's not well. There's this feeling that something is very wrong, but what? What happened to our idyllic life?"

Without warning, I recalled when we first arrived in Scotland. This place had been Thomas's dream for such a long time. After the incident with Uncle Robert and his lies, my husband began to binge-read about Scotland, especially old Scotland, when wolves and lynx roamed the hillsides. Invariably, he referred to a land of "his" past. After a while, I longed to live in this place that held our roots—one with silver-colored hills and the bluest of oceans.

I now tightly forced my eyelids together as though that action might aid my mind. I allowed my thoughts to carry me back to the day of our arrival and our first visit to Johnny Foxes Pub. This unique place became our favorite hangout. The Bunchrew House Hotel, where we stayed on our arrival, had recommended it.

"Please, let this more recent memory jolt my mind. What happened on the day I first arrived? Come on, Caroline, you have to remember!"

We had stood at the bar, sharing a pint. "Thom, will we buy a castle similar to the gorgeous hotel where we're staying?"

"Aye, the place we'll live will be the prettiest in Scotland. Ye can take that to the bank, Caroline Emma Corbett Reid, the belle of Charleston and soon to be of Scotland." He kissed me long and hard. I noticed some locals staring at us from the back of the pub. It was fine. We were Americans and dressed a little differently. Yes, we had stayed too long and drank too much. At one point, Thom set his gloinne atop his head and attempted to balance it there as he danced a little jig.

"You look so stupid," I said as I doubled over with laughter.

"Aye, he does. And he's a caileag bhòidheach!"

One of the locals, who had also drunk too much ale, shouted his insult at my husband before trying to kiss me. Thom and I earlier studied Gaelic before arriving; I knew the tall, red-haired stranger meant that I was "a pretty lass." I could smell stale beer and food on his breath, but underneath that was a pleasant, high-dollar cologne.

Naturally, Thom, whom I had never seen get into a fight except for the time he punched his older brother in the eye in a brawl over me, threw a punch at the Scotsman. That proved to be a massive mistake. You never hit a Scot unless you can take his return punch.

Maybe the man reminded him of his brother because Thom laughed the entire time the big Scot pummeled him. Max had red hair, just like the brawler. My husband and I ended up being escorted from the pub but returned the next night. Malcolm, the red-haired patron, was there when we returned. And, eventually, we all became dear friends. Thom and I came to love him.

"Now, what happened to Malcolm?" I couldn't recall. "Where are you, dear friend?" I saw the handsome Scot, but his memory vanished as though something terrible had happened to him. What?

"Malcolm, are you involved in all of this? I prefer to die if you are because I couldn't bear it if you betrayed us. It would kill my husband too if he isn't already dead." *Will all of these loose threads ever weave into a comprehensive story?* Until they did or I died from dehydration, I must allow my mind to ramble over past events.

Chapter Six

About the time Thom began to press me on moving to his beloved Scotland, the land of pristine rivers and snowy mountains, I dreamed of how it looked. When we were nine years old, Thomas's interest in building castles, sandcastles, began. It changed him into a dreamer. He was never the same after creating his first one. Lovingly, I recalled the time we built his initial castle.

"Caroline Emma, do you remember how strong you've always been? Don't you forget the noble past that flows in your blood." Once again, I heard his booming voice inside the cooling room.

"Thom, what's this?" My momma had asked. She flipped through his new book. "An interest in the building process? Well, that's a delightful endeavor. Do you want to be a builder like your father?"

Easy for her to say, "A delightful endeavor" since she hadn't agreed to spend this gorgeous day beside him as he fussed in the sand while every other kid on the beach had fun. This time was our families' first full summer at our new beach homes on Cape San Blas, Florida. I had agreed to spend the day, a hot one, on the beach with my boyfriend, the Reid brother Thomas. Max had dumped me for a raven-haired beauty he proclaimed had a "nicer set." She did. My young chest was concave, but Thom didn't seem to mind. I didn't want to help him but felt it was vital that I demonstrated how committed I was to him. Any girl who spent a day in the sand and flies with a boy building sandcastles had to be either crazy or in love. If he realized my strength and commitment, maybe, he wouldn't trade me in again for a better girl?

"Caroline Emma, you going to help him?" Momma's intense look told me that I had made the right decision in agreeing to this stupid idea.

"Yes, Momma, I can't wait," I lied.

"Okay, I'll sit right here on the porch and watch. You kids can go to the beach but stay right there where Daddy put the big white tent. Do you see it? Okay, build a mansion. Young man, I'm encouraged about your interest in architecture. You will make a nice living and some girl a successful husband." Lovingly, she messed his shining blond hair. He looked a little embarrassed; I felt very humiliated. It was as though Mom had just married us off after learning about the possible hefty money in his future.

Momma handed me a large, red-striped Lancôme bag filled with sunscreen and other beach necessities. A new little sun hat sat on the top, so I pulled on the pretty straw cover, which had a large blue ribbon around the crown. There was also a sizable pair of blue sunglasses that I slid onto my face. Thom took the bag from me and grabbed my right hand.

"You look marvelous!" My future builder smiled. "I'm gonna marry you someday because you're the perfect partner for me, Caroline Emma Corbett."

Southern girls love to use all of their names.

Together, we hurried to the beach. Once there, the blond boy pulled his glistening new book from his swim trunks and opened it to the beginning.

"We aren't going to build just any old sandcastle, my Caroline. We are building a giant one."

I shuddered. This project could take all summer. We were far enough away from the tide that, unfortunately, nothing would disrupt our work. Thom opened the book as I longingly studied the water.

"Look, Thom, there's a pod of dolphins! Want to go watch them?"

He didn't even look my way. "Ah, nope, thanks, building sandcastles is difficult to work, Caroline. I have to stay focused."

I hoped that the Reid family might return soon with Elizabeth Eisenhour. The whole family had driven Max to pick up his girlfriend, who looked like a dark-haired miniature Dolly Parton. I hated her. She was now Max's true love. I bet Thomas would be ready to desert his project once the "nice set" arrived. At my age, boobs were a big deal for girls. I hopefully looked down at my chest, but there were no changes to report since my last inspection. My chest always appeared to curve inward.

An eternity passed as my future husband groaned over his book. "Okay, I think I've picked the best castle for us to start."

We'd sat in the fluffy white sand for over an hour and had yet to begin building. Even with the tent that Daddy provided, the sand was hot. My great builder walked around a piece of the beach and studied it from every angle. I was dying in the heat, and the flies were starting to bite me. Once they taste your blood, they never give up until you've killed them. I loyally remained glued in place and swatted my body so hard that the hits left little red streaks.

"Okay, we need to dig a moat that is eight feet in diameter." No sooner had these orders left his mouth than I sprang into action.

I was wilting from the heat. "Okay, I'll begin here." With my trusty shovel, I began to dig.

"Oh, no, not there, I've planned it here. Right, here is where we need to dig for eight feet. Yes, right here, sorry about that, Caroline, you made a good start, but I believe it's better located back here."

Thom turned and waved at Mom, who returned his wave with a giant smile but immediately continued to read her glossy magazine. She appeared cool and relaxed in the shade. *Where is Daddy? Why doesn't he rescue me from this hell?*

My lovely French braid fell limply around my face. *What is it about the Reid boys that cause me to end up looking limp and haggard every time I'm in their presence?* I knew that I tried too hard, but that was me.

"Okay, now we take this volcano and make a bowl in the center. See, Caroline, like this." Skillfully, he shaped the sand as if he had performed this process many times.

Thom's demonstration was throwing sand down my swimsuit top. At least, it gave me some volume. I was digging like a maniac —anything to make this torture session end.

"Great, you see how nice this looks?"

All I saw was a pile of sand. This entire day was hopeless. Once again, the love of my limited life glared at his shiny book that was now stained with watermarks and filled with sand, sort of like my chest.

"Now, what was that ratio of water to sand? I thought I had that all worked out." His blond head again lowered into the ragged book.

I thought I might cry. What is happening, brain surgery without the brains? Even the thought of spending the day with Elizabeth Eisenhour seemed tempting compared to this.

"Okay, now we build the topple-proof tower. I'll do this because it requires a bit of delicacy. You start the additions that are built with sand pancakes. I'll show you how to do those."

Thom leaned in close to me. I wanted so much to kiss him. His skin was already bronzed from the sun and glistened with sweat. He was a magnificent boy. Out of nowhere, I thought of dear Josey.

Confident that I now suffered from heatstroke, once again, I almost cried. The heat was horrific, and the yellow flies were miserable. One flew down the top of my pretty blue swimsuit, now smeared with sand and sweat. When that sucker bit me, I screamed in pain. It felt like a mouthful of teeth anchored onto my delicate skin. If I didn't have the beginning of boobs, at least I would have several swollen insect bites to enhance my sensitive young chest. I was almost crying in misery but refused to abandon my true love. I refuse to leave him.

Then a light I had never seen before shined out of those giant brown eyes. Thom appeared transformed by the sight of this monstrosity of sand before us.

Consistently, he had praised our work. I turned my body away from him, hoping that I might catch a breeze coming from the north, but I was wrong. The only thing coming from that direction was another swarm of yellow flies. Josey would have stormed the beach and demanded that I eat and drink something.

Mom remained glued to her chair in the shade of the balcony, reading another magazine. Earlier, I noticed that she left for a few minutes. I hoped it was to prepare lunch for Thom and me, but no, she carried a giant glass of lemonade when she reappeared. Apparently, she had eaten without a thought for her only child who languished beside her true love out of loyalty and the need to demonstrate to him that she would never abandon him. No matter how stupid and vain his actions, I would stick to him like glue.

When I saw Daddy, I thought help was near, that there was sanity in our home. Surely he is coming to tell Thom and me that we must go inside out of the heat and that onslaught of mosquitoes and flies. But, to my amazement, he praised my companion and his "magnificent castle."

"Wow, Thomas. I just learned from Mrs. Reid that you plan to be an architect. That true, son? Well, I've been wondering who I could pass on my hardware store to someday, and I guess it's you. Yes, siree, you and I will work side-by-side. I'll teach you all about the hardware industry. We'll erect shopping malls, bridges, hotels; you name it. With your designs and my supplies, we'll be unstoppable. How does that sound? Oh, hi, Caroline, woo-hoo, you stink, honey. You need a long bath. Why don't you run on up to the house and do that? You're a mess."

At last, what I prayed for earlier had occurred, but his words were more of a suggestion than an order, so I remained glued to Thomas. Things became so uncomfortable that I thought briefly of my best friend, Paula Peterson, and the peaceful place where she now resided. I had never visited her grave, but in the past few hours, I considered how fortunate she was to escape the hell I was enduring. Anything seemed better than this.

I stood, prepared to run to the house if I could still move. Cramps gripped my withered legs because I had sat for so long, making dumb sand patties or pancakes or some such thing. I made so many that they grouped around Thomas in a large circle. A refreshing glass of lemonade called me. I smiled with such love at Daddy.

"Caroline, where do you think you're going? You can't leave this young lad here, alone, to complete his first masterpiece. Just look at what the two of you have done! This structure is quite magnificent."

When I turned to look, I gasped in amazement. Stretching before me was an incredible tour de force of moats and towers. The steeples appeared suspended over graceful minarets. This creation was the most astonishing thing I had ever seen.

The blond boy looked at me with such love and respect. I believed, at that moment, he knew! *He realizes that I am indeed trustworthy and will never leave him. No matter the discomfort or pain, I will remain by his side. We are soulmates.*

Also, at that same moment, I realized that I had lost Daddy. He now precisely considered me to be what I thought of myself, a vessel for Thomas Baxter Reid. His young daughter became the attraction that would procure the perfect ending to his story. It was true. Often, he discussed his fears that I would never be able to run his booming business. Not because of my gender, but the fact that I had no interest in the hardware industry. Now, Thom Reid had just saved his dreams. I would be sacrificed as a helpmate for this person who also loved the building process. Daddy's relief was the thought of all the beautiful projects he would help my handsome husband build with his store as the backer. Although Thom's way of honoring his gift was the actual design, he should understand the building process quickly and need plenty of Daddy's materials. Life now made sense to my father, not because of the talents of Mom and me, but because of my neighbor, the gorgeous Mr. Reid.

At that moment, a truth of extreme consequences landed on my sweaty shoulders. *I love a dreamer. My future husband isn't like any of the others.* Briefly, my thoughts stopped as I succumbed to exhaustion

Chapter Seven

When I awakened, a small bird stood on the windowsill. It looked like a house sparrow. He was tiny with a brown body and a little white chest. The miniature creature turned his head as he studied me. Thirst consumed me, but I no longer felt the pangs of hunger.

"Well, hello, dear friend. I wish I could feed you, but, you see, I'm starving. There's no food here. You've replaced the raging fire as my best friend. I wish that you could take me away. Can you end this madness? What happened to that hot day on the beach at Cape San Blas?" I looked frantically around as though I might see it.

Instead, the sounds of the forest touched my ears. These weren't the early morning sounds that I loved, but like those at the end of the day. *Is darkness upon me? So, I've lain here two days now?* It felt like a week. I wasn't sure of the days or of the time.

Longingly, I recalled an earlier pattern with my husband as we enjoyed the initial morning sound of birds. We frequently rose before sunrise. The peaceful calls of many different species sounded like a gentle symphony. I supposed that my visitor had prompted this thought. As the sun continued to rise, the bird sounds grew with intensity until suddenly, there was quiet. That was our favorite time of the day. Those peaceful times usually created deep joy for Thom and me.

Finally, Mother Nature called, and I couldn't help myself. The hot sensation of fluid flowed under my body. For as long as I could bear it, I had held it until I felt that my bladder might burst. The paper I wrote years earlier for a writing class again came to mind. I recalled that the average person makes 1,500 milliliters of urine every twenty-four hours while the average human bladder can only hold 400-600 milliliters of liquid. Either I was Superwoman or confused in my perception of the time. Of course, I had consumed neither food nor water during my incarceration. *What difference does it make?* The humiliation of feeling the warm fluid caused me to cry. The room felt a little cooler, but the wet sheets felt warm, at least for a while. It helped. My body felt numb, and not much mattered except for a powerful thirst. I would have licked the sheets if I had been able.

My mind involuntarily returned to a time of peace and comfort as Josey and I stood together. We packed Momma's things after her sudden death from cancer. I held one of my mother's favorite dresses close to my chest. It was blue, the same color as the shift I now wore while tied to my bed. I had sniffed Momma's dress. Her perfume, Shalimar, still clung to it. Tears slowly dripped from my eyes on that earlier day, just like today, after I wet the bed. I was worried back then about leaving Daddy, even though the Reid family, Thomas's family, still lived next door. They and Josey would look after him as my husband, and I moved to his dreamland. *Always, there was Josey.* I held up the sky-blue dress in front of Momma's full-length gilt mirror as that special day floated across my memory.

Dreamily, I had spun before Momma's mirror while I recalled an extraordinary event where I also had twirled in the dress of an angel inside Thom's arms. I almost didn't attend the St. Cecilia Society Ball, but I changed my mind because of Josey's encouragement. I would be forever grateful that she had insisted I go and had explained to me the importance of something that I once thought trivial.

Four days before Christmas, the Annual Debutante Ball occurred in Charleston. I was nervous. Our dance was famous, although Savannah, our competitor, held the title as the "Oldest Ball." Their first event was celebrated in 1817, and ours in 1822.

"Well, that's about the only edge old Savannah has over us." Marilyn Povey, the daughter of the most prominent physician in Charleston, cooed those words as we all laughed.

The Ball was an essential event in my Southern town of wealth and beauty. The women presented were the most sought after and accomplished in the area. You can't imagine all of the lavish decorations and fuss! As we met at 8:00 p.m., eerie quietness fell over our small group. Probably because we couldn't believe this particular night had finally arrived. Preparations in anticipation of it had occurred for over a year. The weather could not have been more welcoming, but the beautiful young women still ran for the protection of our stunning surroundings. We had to look perfect, not a hair out of place.

There were only two times in our history that the Ball didn't take place. During both the Civil War and World War II, it was canceled. That should stress the importance it held in our city. On my special evening, everyone hurried immediately to the ballroom to watch the procession of lovely ladies. My inclusion in such an honored and prestigious event made me proud.

I thought my gown was the most lavish. My shimmering white charmeuse frock took months to create. When I finally pulled it gently over my body, the fit was perfect. I'll never forget the luxuriant way it felt when I whirled before the mirror, just like when I later held up Momma's blue dress in front of her mirror. My designer laughed and applauded! Momma cried. The feeling that came over me created great humility. It felt like an out-of-body experience. That's how powerful being a debutante feels to young women like me. And at that moment, I realized my entitlement.

Elizabeth and I stood side by side. We were both dressed in full-length, sleeveless white gowns with long white gloves. I hoped I projected just a fraction of the beautiful aura rolling in waves off the raven-haired Elizabeth, whom Max escorted. The Reid boys looked extraordinary! Both Thom and Max wore full dress white tie and tails with white gloves. Each of them took my breath away! Never had the brothers been so handsome. Everyone swooned when they strutted past. They were the most attractive men Charleston had to offer.

All the debs wore white designer gowns. Our hair swept up and off our faces and held with elaborate hair jewelry. As a surprise, my father presented me with a gorgeous gold comb before my hair appointment. Momma and I had rushed to my hairdresser on that long-ago evening. Martha, my stylist, oohed and aahed the entire time she designed an elaborate hairdo held in place by Daddy's brilliant gift. I didn't even look like myself. Mom started to cry when she saw me. Thank goodness she had to rush me home to dress, or I would have sobbed and messed my makeup.

In the spring of that year, Elizabeth and I had attended a formal tea, but that in no way could have prepared us for THE big night. My hands were perspiring as Thom gently held them. I felt grateful for the white gloves that we both wore. Friends and families lined the edge of the ballroom floor while we waltzed with our handsome escorts. I hoped that I wouldn't drop anything on my gown since this event also highlighted our social graces. Each of the debutantes received a bouquet of twelve red roses tied with long red satin streamers. They were exquisite.

When the selection process first began, I had feared rejection. It took over a year for completion of the procedure, which haunted my nights. And a girl could never be certain of receiving an invitation. I can genuinely say that this process changed my life. Once I received notification that I was selected, my boyfriend's chest swelled with pride. For over a year, Mom and I planned my look down to the perfect handbag, even though I never carried it. The roses were my anchor. I thanked God again for the gloves, so the handsome blond man didn't feel my sweaty hands as I smiled up into those warm chocolate eyes of his.

While Thom and I glided and swayed around the ballroom floor, I looked into his eyes, those of the man I loved, who was different from any other. All of our lives we had been inseparable, except for the brief time he "loved" Paula Peterson, the short times he and Max tag-teamed each other as my boyfriend, and the four years of separation during college.

I often wondered if Thom might have known somehow that Paula's life would be cut short, and for a while, he wanted to make it special. Of course, I never asked him anything so strange. Still, I believed it. You see, I had come to believe that Thomas Baxter Reid was an angel. He would accomplish remarkable things. Without a doubt, I knew that his actions on this earth would change the planet, even if only in a small way. He would try. I had no idea of the depth of those beliefs. Also, I would later be staggered by his noble deeds.

"Caroline Emma, you take my breath away. I almost added Reid on there." He smiled.

There was a loud buzzing in my ears as I watched girls around me whom I'd known all my life, sway to the music. *They all look like angels.* "Hmm? What did you say? Reid?"

"That's right; I forgot, for a moment, that we aren't married. I almost called you Caroline Emma Reid."

He smelled divine. Many times, I felt tempted to give myself to him in the past, but this small, still voice inside whispered, "Don't do it. He's a special man. Make him wait for a special gift." We had yet to consummate our relationship.

"Oh, how I love the sound of that. Say it again, Thom."

Again, he whispered, "Caroline Emma Corbett Reid."

We danced a little too close, and I saw Momma shake her head. *Better not offend the ladies of the club.* Faster and faster, my love spun me around the room. Everything and everyone became a blur, blending in with the apricot walls. I threw my head back with abandon for being allowed to feel the joy of entitlement. Someday, we would give back to this world, which had bestowed so many blessings upon us.

And when others called us selfish, we would know in our souls the price we paid for these wonderful lives. Luke 12:48 says, "For unto whomsoever, much is given, of him shall be much required." *What will God require of us?* I wondered at that time. Tonight, I knew it would be my life.

Chapter Eight

The fire's size and intensity had waned even more inside my beautiful prison. A cold shiver ran down my spine. The Willow Room in Alladale already felt very chilly, and I could sense the temperature falling quickly. Once more, fear gripped me when I considered my fate and what apparently waited for me.

"Thom, we did give back. Together, we have accomplished more than I ever dreamed possible. I don't want to leave our lives, but I don't want to continue without you. Please, come for me one more time. Either in death or life, but, please, let us end it together. Dear God, is that what you will require of me to finish my life without him?" *I don't think that I can.*

Maybe, the chills are a sign that I'm dying? It no longer mattered. It seemed as if, while I remembered memories in Charleston, similar actions occurred here, at Alladale. *Oh, how I wish I might wear that luxurious snow-white gown again. I can feel the rich fabric. But this place isn't Charleston. No, I'm in my beloved adopted home of Scotland.*

My body ached. My mind was exhausted from my three trains of thought: everlasting memories from beloved Charleston, my childhood home; later events in Scotland; and the desperation I felt in trying to understand my current situation. It was all too much. Tears added to my blurry vision, and I wished they would wash away the haze. They didn't, but I sank deeper into the down mattress, which suspended my body. Lights flashed into the room, pulling me from my thoughts. *Is that my killer finally coming for me?* The bed shook as I imagined how I might eventually die. Again, I tried to slide farther under the covers, but it was still impossible.

Don't give in to fear! You must be strong. Remember, think happy thoughts. "Is that you, my love? Are you here? I'm so glad!" I heard a distant sound! *It must be Thom!* My attempt to sit up in the bed proved disastrous. I felt ridiculous. How many times would I pull on the thick metal cuffs around my wrists and ankles? They only chafed my skin and caused it to bleed.

I questioned if I had genuinely lost it when the meaning of a slightly strange Gaelic word waffled into my mind, "dreicht." That was Thomas's favorite saying to the staff when they did something wrong or funny. He used it in a manly way, more of a joke. The word meant "defeat" in English. He had learned Gaelic so easily. When we first came to Scotland, it surprised me to hear the language roll from the locals' tongues. Over 60,000 Scots spoke that language. It was beloved here. The style never defeated Thomas, but I appeared destined to struggle with it.

There were no more sounds. Only silence filled my beloved Alladale. "Oh, my love, where are you?"

Tears continued to roll off my face onto the top of my soft blue linen shift with little embroidered flowers. The color reminded me of Momma's dress when Josey and I packed her clothes after her death. Is this another link? Am I wearing the color which I link with Momma's death? No logic existed. Nothing made sense.

"Are these flowers embroidered on my shift, heather?"

It felt too coincidental that I lay bound to my bed in a blue shift the same color as the blue pot of heather sitting beside me, and the same flowers stitched into the material of my dress. If not coincidental or totally illogical, was this a well-planned scheme to drive me deeper into insanity?

The fresh wetness of my bed made me cry again, but I couldn't help myself. Any attempt to remain human, any wish to feel normal was long gone. Now, it was easy to let the urine flow.

My tears of humiliation added to the crust around my eyes. It was harder to open them. They felt swollen and matted closed.

The burning smell of ammonia irritated my nostrils. I stared at the pretty pot of heather with their little pink-purple heads through scratched eyes. How quickly I had lost any pretense; any feelings of entitlement had been stripped away by the uncontrollable body forces. It was God and me against whoever this was that meant to humiliate and probably kill me.

My mind raced as though I could stop what was coming if I could only figure out my life. There was a fight, a brawl, happening in my mind.

I stood with my husband on a snowy hilltop. Alladale was ours at last. We had no idea that we would eventually turn this spectacular place into a 23,000-acre nature reserve, refurbish the two lodges, and build two new cottages. All we knew was that this place had stolen our hearts.

When I almost drifted away, a sudden bolt of adrenaline rushed through my veins. "If only I could get out of this bed. I have to find my husband. And what about the house? Is everything okay?" Again, I tugged on the shackles that held my hands. More blood trickled down my wrists from the broken skin. "Let me see, I've peed in the bed, bled in the bed, and lost my mind in the bed." I felt so tired. "Please, God, just end it here, now! Please."

Quickly, I realized it wasn't Momma before me, only her image. The face of my beloved mother had replaced that of my husband. I believed Momma visited me there, in my darkest hour, as had my dear husband.

Her earlier words about marriage rang in my ears. "Caroline Emma, I wish that I could give you the wisest words in the world to guide you in your marriage, but I don't have any. My suggestion is to let your husband be the man. He's a Scot, you know. We all know. Don't corner him. Be gentle when you advise him. He adores you. The life he provides you will surpass your wildest dreams if you can hold your tongue. When you plant two Scots in the same garden, that's cause for a problem." I felt her gentle kiss brush my cheek.

"Was I a good wife? I know, I didn't want to leave Charleston, and we fought savagely for a while." My question hung unanswered in the air.

"I'm not in Charleston. Ahhh, I'm back in Alladale. Everything keeps changing. I can't keep up with it. My beautiful home where Thom and I shared such joy. Alladale, how can you allow this to happen to me? We loved you. We restored you. Help me, please!"

Once more, I jerked my wrists, and the bleeding started again. I considered the sheets on which I lay, soaked in urine and blood. *What else waits for me?* I was losing control of my body. *Is this the end, at last?* I no longer feared the end but prayed that I might receive a second chance at life, although it seemed impossible.

The little pink-purple flowers in the pretty blue pot now looked absurd. "I hate you!" I yelled into the night as their cute little heads drooped from lack of water. They, too, were dying. When I saw that the flowers had wilted, I felt rage. Anger boiled within me. *Not only am I about to die, but he or she killed the beautiful flowers.*

"Where are you, you maniac? Come and release me. I'll tell my husband. He'll take care of you." For a brief moment, I felt prepared to fight.

Early on, I told myself that if I was to endure this, I must be strong. There was no room for cowards. *I won't cry, nor will I feel sorry for myself.* Instead, I'll let my mind move me back to a happy time when all of Thom's dreams of Scotland began, but I wasn't yet aware of his love for the building and designing process. We had no idea where his ambitious goals would carry us.

Chapter Nine

Daddy's reaction to my leaving Charleston wasn't what I had expected. After Momma's death, he smiled and played a little golf with his buddies, but he wasn't the same. A part of him had also died. The doctors told me that after her death, he suffered a small stroke. There weren't any visible physical signs, but it caused slowness in his rational responses.

Uncle Robert's antics hadn't helped. On our departure day, knowing that we were leaving for an unknown period, I dreaded stopping by the wedding-cake house, which I loved, to kiss Daddy and Josey goodbye. My family and that of the Reids had decided the night before, as we gathered at the club for dinner, to end the chapter there. Yet, I had to stop and see Daddy once more.

"Now, Caroline, you phone when you arrive. Don't worry about Josey and me. We'll be fine. Remember, this is your life. Yours and Thomas's, so make it count."

Daddy had seldom given me words of encouragement. Those came from Momma. Even Josey's composure amazed me. Once we left, I figured they would fall apart, but it helped that they didn't in front of us. Daddy said a few words to Thomas in private. I never asked, and Thom never told me what was said. Today, I wished I knew those words Daddy had spoken.

We had several options for flying but decided to rent a car and drive to Atlanta, then fly on British Airways. I enjoyed the luxury they provided. Weeks earlier, we had sold our home furnished and our cars to some friends who always loved them. Mrs. Reid would send the clothes and personal items we'd packed after we found a home. All the loose ends connected with such ease that it surprised me. It felt like a letdown.

Once we were in the air, I felt disappointed that there had been so little drama. "Caroline, you just can't be happy," I said in a whisper to myself.

It startled me when those beautiful chocolate eyes stared at me. "What? Caroline, did you just say you aren't happy?" Thom looked appalled, so did I that I had dared to say such a thing.

"No, of course not, I've never been happier. Bring on the adventure. Inverness, here we come!" I laughed with a nervous giggle.

I had no idea why I said this negative statement, except I already missed Momma, and now Daddy, Josey, and the beautiful wedding-cake house. *Can we ever find anything that would fill the place of my childhood home that held such enchanting memories?*

We tapped our champagne glasses, followed by another kiss. The flight was comfortable and without problems. It took about twelve hours. *Thom and I are young, so that we won't suffer much from jet lag.* At least that's what I thought in the beginning. My husband had taken care of all of the reservations, which explained why there were no problems.

My first step onto Scottish soil occurred on June 6, our first wedding anniversary. We thought that by doing this, we wouldn't forget our date with destiny in Scotland once we were old and gray. I couldn't have known that the two of us would never share old age. As the plane landed in Dalcross, I could barely breathe due to the anxiety of living in a new place. I had never changed towns during my life of twenty-three years. Even when I attended the College of Charleston, I hadn't left that fair city.

I heard many different languages around me because Dalcross was an international airport. Everything felt rural; I loved it. Inverness sat on Scotland's northeastern coast, where the Ness River flowed into the Moray Firth. I found the area breathtaking.

"When can we explore castles and find our home?" My handsome husband smiled at my innocent question.

It seemed to take a long time to collect our luggage and locate our rental car, but time was all we had. Our drive from Dalcross to the hotel filled me with longing and anticipation. Our "home away from home" stood proudly on the water.

Thomas loved the hotel. "Caroline, maybe we should buy this. Is it big enough for ye, me lady?" He began to cite all sorts of historical facts. I knew that he had studied "all things Scotland" for years, but his knowledge impressed me.

When he pronounced Bunchrew, he said, "Buncrieve." My proud Scot husband belonged in this place. He explained that Bunchrew meant "the root of the tree" or "the wooded slope." My love fascinated me with Alexander of Lovat's stories, the original owner when the house had only two rooms in 1505. I didn't expect much. However, as he turned into this romantic and famous place, I hoped we never found our estate. It seemed impossible that we would be living there for months, maybe years. I had never lived in a hotel but always considered that it would be glamorous. I thought of Hemingway and F. Scott Fitzgerald with Zelda in Paris. *Perhaps, Caroline Emma Corbett Reid might pen a great novel here?* I hoped that our room looked over the water. How can I ask for more inspiration than this?

"Can we visit the Battlefield of Culloden?" I thought my question might impress any patrons standing around the lobby of the stately hotel. Thomas just smiled at me while he checked us into the room. I guessed my husband knew me too well.

A nice-looking older gentleman, who sported a fuzzy white mustache on his upper lip, smiled broadly at us. It was the color of white silk and matched his hair. That mustache didn't look real, and I wanted to touch it to see. He wore a dark blue checked jacket with dark blue trousers. He was a dandy.

"Ya better well visit it! It's located right there." He pointed behind my head. "If ya stay here, watch out for ghosts. Don't ye young people be saying I'm bacach, 'cause I'm not. See that, over there? That hill? It's famous, ya know. That's Craig Dunain!

If ya see a red-haired girl, well, ye'll know the end is near."

The maniacal laughter from his old mouth frightened me.

Thomas laughed, so I figured those words weren't meant for my ears. The stranger shook a fancy cane with a golden eagle's head at us and pranced away. Several people were standing at the entrance of the place. I rushed after him, but he seemed to disappear into the crowd. There wasn't a sign of him.

Thomas looked at me and laughed. "Bacach means lame. What the rest means, well, I have no idea. Ya'll get used to it. It may be a phrase that's passed around. For sure, he didn't coin it."

I doubted it, but I already loved the place. No longer did I fear the change and the apprehension that I might not fit into this place of warriors and ghosts because all of my life, I dreamed of such.

A handsome young Scotsman was assigned to escort us to our rooms. He was very young and quite thin, with a bright, contagious smile. The bellhop dressed in a dark blue blazer with gray slacks; his white shirt appeared to glow in the light of the sconces on the wall. He smiled at me as he pointed out a tall window. The boy-man appeared to be very interested in us. I figured that he realized we were American.

"Thomas, I notice that the rooms don't have numbers." He and the attendant good-naturedly laughed.

"Aye, our rooms are named after local places and Scottish clans." When the handsome young man opened the door to our suite, I gasped.

"The suites in this hotel were all 4-star, so I imagined they were all impressive. I hope ye like ours!" Thomas looked around us in awe.

"Are you kidding me? This space is our room for how long? It must be the best suite in the hotel."

"Aye, madam, this is the only one with a flaming gas fire. If you are here this winter, you'll be happy you chose this beauty. Many brides request it."

I ran to the window, which featured a breathtaking view of Beauly Firth. This suite also provided a conservatory where I pictured myself enjoying a cup of tea on the window seat's thick cushions while I gazed at the sea waters. Today, they were gray because of the turbulence. The wind howled.

The color palette of pale golds and sage greens, with a splattering of terra cotta red, surrounded me. *Those colors within the rooms please me.* And the location on the ground floor was ideal for quick changes as we rushed to meet builders and planned our new home.

My husband planted a generous wad of bills into the hand of the young Duncan Abernathy. "Now, I think a nap's a-callin' me." With a twinkle in his eye and a tilt in his kilt, my husband slowly closed the door. *I think he plans more than a nap!*

Chapter Ten

Thoughts of the day we arrived in Scotland, after the brawl in Johnny Foxes, came to mind. Maybe we did suffer from jet lag, or too much ale, or a combination of the two, but we fell into our down-filled bed, exhausted after being asked to leave the pub. Neither of us had ever been thrown out of a place of business. I wondered if this might be a sign of trouble in our futures.

Tiredness had seeped into every fiber of our bodies. Thom snored in contentment, or maybe he passed out. Sadly, my thoughts turned to how much Uncle Robert had caused Daddy and Thom to suffer.

When my young, blond boy returned home to Charleston, after becoming an architect of some renown, he was considered the "golden boy" of the town. But after months of Uncle Robert's lies and accusations, both Daddy's business and Thom's suffered significant hits. Some long-term customers chose to believe the smear campaign of a bitter and angry family member. All of it hurt Thomas. My daddy was older and had gone through Robert's games before, but Thom hadn't. Deep in my heart, I believed that to be the catalyst that spurred his desire to leave Charleston for a fresh start.

However, after his battle with my uncle, he didn't have the old fire about designing that he once possessed. I hoped that it would return soon; after all, he had promised to build the castle of my dreams. Everything that I loved and held dear to my heart was left behind because of my husband's promises. Now, what would happen if he was burned out and unable to deliver? It wouldn't matter in my heart because I loved him so much, but it would greatly disappoint both of us.

On that day of our arrival in our new home, I lay quietly watching the face of the man I adored. He looked at me, toward the sea. I faced the wall behind him. The sound of calling seabirds filled the world outside. The window remained slightly open so that I could smell the salty fragrance. I licked my lips. *Do I taste it?*

My husband was handsome in sleep and awake. He already sported a gentle tan, which I'd noticed made his dark eyes appear to glow. His hair was streaked with lighter gold and looked professionally colored, but I told him that God fashioned his hair. He loved that.

A new start in a new country, what more could we want? As much as I loved my wedding-cake home, maybe my personal architect could construct something that pleased me. Indeed, nothing could be prettier than my childhood home. Briefly, a vision of the shining white house sprang up before me.

Our house wasn't the largest in Charleston. That boast of fame split between two giants: a famous one that stood ten times larger than the average American home at 20,000 square feet, while the famous Calhoun Mansion boasted 24,000 square feet. My house also didn't contain five hundred pounds of cannon lodged in an attic beam like the stately William Roper House at 9 East Battery. Some homeowners in the 1800s also owned large plantation homes in the country. Many places, which still stand on The Battery today, were second homes. The locals referred to them as "beach cottages," no matter their enormous size.

Will I ever stop pining for Charleston? One minute, excitement charged through me at the thought of this new place. The next, I felt tears in my eyes.

Longingly, I recalled my history within those familiar walls of brick and stone and the delightful, eccentric residents. They always produced a smile in the Southern coastal town that I loved.

My crisp white antebellum home shined like a beacon in my memory. Imagine a house that resembles a wedding cake, and you have it! A tall, shiny black wrought-iron gate shielded our courtyard, those many years ago, and still does, from curious eyes. We got together in the evenings with the Reids and many others. Our Southern beauty showcased a rotunda on whose balcony we spent long nights playing Charades and sipping pink lemonade. I know it sounds corny, but that was us.

Most of the interior rooms displayed various shades of white, showcasing shiny alabaster marble floors and bright antique brown doors. The door handles were all polished brass with different designs carved into a brilliant texture. The massive moldings and baseboards featured gargoyles and creatures from the deep. Let me tell you, at night; this place would frighten even the bravest of souls. In some of those old houses, tales existed that ghosts strolled the long, silent halls. In the evenings, Thom and I waited for hours while our parents chuckled and traded barbs downstairs. We never witnessed any such thing in our two places.

"Aye, Scotland, ye also possess a history of ghosts and pirates. Don't ye look so smug." My torture chamber sadly echoed my empty words.

Immediately, I continued my earlier train of thought as I was transported to Charleston. Six working fireplaces remained in my old beauty, which was rather unusual that they still worked. My favorite room was our kitchen. Rows of shiny mahogany cabinets gleamed in the morning sun as the brown and tan marble counters reflected my image over orange specks. Next, the best room was the rotunda. That's where Thom and I usually spent hours as we watched the passing traffic, both cars and pedestrians. Of course, I generally practiced my ballet moves there.

Each time I entered Thom's home, the golden house, I smelled the distinctive scents of furniture polish and fresh flowers. Mrs. Reid was a fanatic about flowers. Every other day, their maid, Matilda, changed the vases and added clean water and new blooms. Later, I learned that Josey took them from their trash, and, with a little pruning, she was proudly able to display them in her apartment at the foot of the stairs.

At the Reid home, the back courtyard looked like a florist's shop, with massive plantings emerging from old magnolia trees and ancient shrubs that continued to flower each year. Such incredible beauty took my breath away as I tried to imagine an age of such magnificence. Even dazzling, fragile orchids peeped from secret places in the old mossy trees. My mom used to say she thought that Mrs. Reid peed on the plants to get them to grow so high. I never had the nerve to ask her, but Thom told me that he and Max relieved themselves often in the garden. Something increased the size and luxurious green color of their vegetation!

Behind Thom's house, a large swimming pool always waited for us. It received a massive workout many months of the year. Oh, the secrets we shared! I couldn't remember all of the parties we enjoyed. My parents refused to consider installing a pool at our Charleston home, but when we purchased our beach house, they installed one there. Thom also had several fireplaces inside his august residence. Just like ours, they all worked, which Daddy said was "most unusual."

The Reid's home, that famous house of gold, also held many memories. Of course, it wasn't real gold, but in the evenings with the sunset, Thom's house blazed in a golden glow. I loved to climb the broad steps to his massive front porch. Two sets of stairs split on each side of the entrance. Enormous antique windows shined, and dark green shutters highlighted them while glowing white moldings flanked the entire residence. Satiny white columns shielded sparkling antiques of immense beauty inside.

I always knew that Thomas Reid was a great architect, but had the pain caused by Uncle Robert affected him so profoundly that he might not be able to design again? I had heard of such things. It was the dinner hour; I felt famished but refused to awaken my love after the long flight to Scotland and our banishment from the bar.

Quietly, I thought more about Charleston and Daddy while I continued to stare at my husband. *Is my father eating alone at the great table in the dining room? Does he miss me?* I wondered if he still cried for Momma. I did. Since Momma's death, Josey had insisted that he have new long-tapered white candles each evening just like Momma had loved. He poo-pooed her idea, but no one could stop Josey. Sadly, the image of him looking around the gorgeous wedding-cake house, where all his dreams came to life, made me sad. *Will I someday sit at a massive table in a great home, here in Scotland, alone?*

It felt like I should be able to hear the early evening sounds from the Charleston streets. The Battery would be busy at this hour, with many people strolling the shore. I listened intently, but there was only silence inside Alladale.

My beautiful, beloved Charleston began in 1670; it was named Charles Towne in honor of King Charles II of England. Although founded on the West bank of Albemarle Point by the Ashley River, that site, called Charles Towne Landing, was initially abandoned after a few years. Soon, the town was re-established at the present location in 1680. Because of the port location and beautiful area, it quickly grew to be the fifth-largest city in North America within five years.

Another major factor in the early rapid growth of the area was the role of the city in the slave trade. This history placed a tarnished spot on a past filled with Southern tradition. An extensive business of selling slaves began in the eighteenth century. At the close of the Revolutionary War, Charles Towne changed the spelling to Charleston with its incorporation into a city in 1783.

Through the early years, Charleston remained the only antebellum American City, with a majority of the population enslaved. This highly successful town was controlled by an oligarchy of white planters and merchants who forced the Federal government to revise its tariffs. When the city seized the Arsenal, Castle Pinckney, and Fort Sumter from federal garrisons, the Civil War began.

Today, when you enter Charleston Harbor, a white cross stands on a small island where prisoners of war stayed during the Civil War. This memorial marks the location of Castle Pinckney, which began as a small masonry fortification built by the US government in 1810. In 2018, the city apologized to the nation for its role in the American Slave Trade. The South remained riddled with such history. Charleston didn't stand alone, but enormous strides had been made not to erase the horrible history but to tell honestly the story of a different time. Briefly, I considered the history of slavery that Scotland possessed; although not as gruesome as that in Charleston, there existed a history.

Travel & Leisure Magazine ranked Charleston as the "Best City in the World." Such has been the fair city's rank by many over the years. My ancestors were among the first to settle the area. The same hardware store that my father proudly started long ago. Of course, it had grown tremendously, and today was modernized.

The term "Charleston Battery" was derived because it once housed several cannons that protected the houses and the city proper. If you strolled down Battery Street, every step moved you two hundred years backward. Breathing the lush freshness of honeysuckle and jasmine, tourists attempted to sound like Scarlett O'Hara, even if they weren't Southern. These folks looked ridiculous as they tried to transform themselves into wealthy plantation owners of the past.

"Charleston, please take care of Daddy and Josey." Sadly, I whispered my plea into the empty, cold room inside of Alladale.

Deep in my heart, I questioned what I had done by leaving them, but I recalled Daddy's words that this was "our life," mine and Thomas's. I felt a tear trickle down my right cheek as someone knocked gently on our door.

Who knocked at our door on that evening of our arrival at the Bunchrew Hotel? From my damp bed in the present, I couldn't recall.

On this night, there were no knocks, only the forest sounds of the approaching darkness. *Have I already lived through the third night?* My head hurt, and lights flashed before my eyes as if fireworks exploded in my head. I thought of Daddy. *Am I having a stroke?* If it produced a quick death, I prayed for it.

Chapter Eleven

Duncan knocked on the door of our suite in the Bunchrew House Hotel. He wore a bright red jacket with a tartan tie.

"Aye, Ms. Caroline, I wanted you to know there are only two fillets of Dover sole remaining. You and Mr. Thom might want to reserve them."

Duncan's giant smile let me know that it must be outstanding. I turned to look at Thomas, who hadn't moved. Usually, he was a light sleeper. Hesitantly, I turned back to face young Duncan, who peered around me.

When he saw my husband, snoring in the bed, he turned red from his redhead, possibly to his feet, which I imagined were fair. I thought of Max. "Oh, Ms. Caroline, I'm sorry. I didn't know you would be, ah—" Again, he blushed as he pointed at the bed.

"Ah, napping?" I laughed.

"Yes, Ms. Caroline, please forgive me, but chef's fish, especially the Dover sole, is legendary. I won't be bothering you again, sorry." He backed away.

Suddenly, Thom jumped from the bed without his pants. He didn't speak; in fact, I thought young Duncan might have a coronary.

"Did he say, Dover sole? Well, save it for us, young Duncan, and yer finest wine." He winked at Duncan, who ran out of the room. We both fell back in hysterics onto the luxurious Egyptian cotton sheets. "I love ya, Caroline."

I awakened with a faint chuckle from the days when we had first arrived in Scotland to the present where I remained in shackles. Briefly, I thought of Josey. If only I had questioned her about her early life and those of her ancestors. It made me sad to realize that I paid so little attention to her past. Slowly, I had become aware of my failures throughout my life. There weren't many that I hadn't considered. *Does this signal the end?*

"Well, none of it matters now, Caroline. Your death awaits. Stop feeling guilty. You can apologize to everyone soon when you arrive in Heaven. I set myself free from guilt!" I shouted into the frigid air before falling into sleep again—or unconsciousness.

"I know, that's why I claimed the shower before ya." I had run into the bathroom to urge Thom to vacate so we could be on time for dinner.

Hopefully, young Duncan has saved the last of the fish for us after all his trouble, I had thought.

About thirty minutes later, we strolled into the downstairs dining room. It surprised me when I noticed that Duncan was waiting tables.

When he saw us, he treated us as if we were old friends. "Aye, I saved it for ya, but chef was about to serve it to the Bairds. They are regulars. Let me run back and alert him that ya still want it. Ya do, don't ya?"

"Want what?" Jet lag had, at last, dimmed my senses. I blinked at the young man who blushed. My head hurt.

"Aye, Duncan, we do!"

Thom slapped him hard on the back, which almost knocked him into an empty table by the door. Duncan looked at my husband with admiration because he was a skinny lad, incapable of ever knocking another man into a table.

Empty tables were at a premium on that night of new beginnings long ago. Frequented by tourists and locals, the hotel was doing a brisk business on that early June evening.

The charming maître d' had escorted us to our reserved table in the back by a window with a view that took my breath away. We spied an island in the distance. "What is that enchanting island?" I pointed.

"Let me see, that would be Black Island." Thom was already poring over the extensive menu. He barely looked at me.

"Are those mountains behind it?"

"They are." His face disappeared behind the menu.

Duncan charged up to us. "Okay, ya got yer fish comin', and I'll bring our finest wine. It's a doozie."

"How would ya know this, young Duncan?" Another blush covered the boy's handsome face from my husband's taunt.

I studied the room as Thom continued to hold the tall menu high in the air. He needed a pair of reading glasses but refused to admit it. I moved the candle closer, hoping the light might help, and he would lower the menu. I was thrilled to think we could enjoy dinner here each evening until we built our castle.

The paneling in the dining room was a lovely wood; I didn't recognize the species. I appreciated the ambiance with the wall sconces dimmed. It suited the place. Darkness had also fallen outside; I realized that we didn't know the time. Far away, the lights of the Kessock Bridge flickered through branches in the gentle wind. I wished never to leave this magical place.

Suddenly, before my eyes, God painted a picture of exquisite beauty. Nothing man built could ever compare. The cloudy night suddenly presented reds, oranges, and purples that were unlike anything I'd ever witnessed.

"God must be pleased with us. Look at the welcome gift he has given us."

From behind the menu, I heard, "Ya mean the gift of young Duncan and his blushing?" He laughed and finally looked at me.

My eyes stared at the spectacle to my right. When my husband turned and saw it, he was so deeply moved that he stood from his chair and placed his hand over his heart. My love appeared mesmerized.

"Aye, Scotland, dearest place, I'm here…there were lovely things in the world, lovely that didn't endure, and the lovelier for that…nothing endures."

Suddenly, many of the men rose and joined him in reciting a large portion of the "Sunset Song," penned by Lewis Grassic Gibbon. I recognized that many considered it an essential Scottish novel of the twentieth century, but many other notable writers hailed from this inspiring land.

When I witnessed Thomas's emotions, I realized that we had done the right thing in leaving Charleston. My husband needed to heal, to return home to his roots. We had done that. Nothing else mattered. Daddy and Josey were right; this was our life, mine, and Thomas's.

Duncan cleared the main course dishes then served a lovely fresh raspberry torte. "Scotland is famous for its soft fruit," he whispered.

"Let me see, ancient architecture, incredible sunsets, handsome fir, pretty lasses, blushing boys, and the best soft fruit. That is remarkable."

"Ya know what's remarkable, Caroline Emma Corbett Reid? That ye agreed to marry me." My husband gently held my right hand.

"Well, if ye recall, this issue was settled when we were five years old. Except for the pause with Paula, I believe our hearts have always belonged to each other."

"Aye, and what is the wish of yer heart, my beauty?" He now caressed my right hand.

I giggled like a schoolgirl when Duncan brought a second bottle of the expensive wine to the table. "I don't believe we ordered this, Duncan."

"Na, ya didn't, but one of the locals sent it to ya. It was Malcolm Dargie. He's a friend to all of us. Ye know him, don't ya?" He nodded toward a huge man with red hair who wore a kilt.

I recognized him as the man in the pub who delivered a purple eye to Thom.

Slowly, he walked toward us, grinning. "I had too much ale the other night. Hope ye'll forgive me. Usually, I don't hit a man I don't know without more cause than with ye, but I lost control." His ample smile revealed perfect sparkling white teeth.

"Aye, I deserved it. Won't ya join us?"

"Na, I won't invade yer space. Looks to me like yer celebrating, maybe, another evening."

It seemed to me that he disappeared into the air. Just like that, he disintegrated. "I didn't see him leave, did you?"

Loudly, Thom laughed as he explained, "Maybe, between the earlier ale and the wine, ye might be seeing things or missing elements. Perhaps," he speculated, "Malcolm joined the white-haired man with the cane. He also disappeared, at least in yer mind." Thom laughingly shook his head at me.

"Well, we might as well finish this bottle. We don't have to drive." A smile from the chocolate eyes greeted my words.

I held out my empty glass to enjoy the same delicious wine Duncan had served earlier. The label was a new one for me. "In answer to your question, my wish is to live in a sandcastle in the snow," I whispered.

Our eyes met. "Can't ya wish for something that I might be able to deliver? How can I design a sandcastle in the snow?" Thom lowered his head.

"Well, how about we shoot for a higher purpose than most others? Lives that accomplish greatness?"

"Aye, now, that I can deliver."

The last thought caused me to leave the past behind as I returned to the damp, cold bed. "Aye, Thom, what we did was magnificent. I'm not afraid of dyin'. I'm afraid of leaving ye."

Thankfully, I fell back into the past.

Chapter Twelve

"Oh, Thomas, what were we thinking? I feel awful. So, this is a hangover? Please, just put me out of my misery. I don't ever want another one. I'm never drinking again." I moaned loudly. *Why isn't he responding?* Again, I groaned with pain. I waited a few seconds, but when he didn't agonize back, I felt his side of the bed. It was empty.

I sat up in the bed, confused. *Have I missed something?* My eyes did a quick inventory of the room. He was gone. Weakly, I stood, but the room spun when I attempted to walk to the toilet. It was impossible to stand upright or to walk a straight line. I listed to the right in a crablike scuttle. I felt sick, which caused me to move as fast as I could. Holding on to the spinning commode, I wondered. *How could Thom have left me in this condition?* When I staggered back to the bed, I saw a note lying on the bedside table. He had hurriedly written: Hate to leave you, but Malcolm stopped by. I'm off with him to look at an available property. See you around lunch.

I held my head as I fell back into bed. *Am I the dumbest person in the world to drink so much? Maybe, I'm dying from alcohol poisoning.* I briefly considered phoning the front desk and asking them to call a doctor, but I decided to wait for Thomas's return. He always came when I needed him. I fell into a deep sleep. My snoring sounded loud, even to me, but I couldn't wake myself.

The thought of a doctor made me recall Dr. Lafferty, my pediatrician, who restored my health from childhood anemia. He had never let me down during my life, nor did he on the occasion before school was scheduled to open in my early days. With only the weekend between me and the beginning of my third grade, Momma was freaking out because we hadn't received word from him about my blood tests for anemia.

"Look, Momma, it's not like I can die from anemia, right? I'm just not feeling well. I believe I can make it to school, okay. Especially since I'm homeschooled in the library downstairs, don't worry. You'll die from a heart attack before I ever die from anemia."

Josey had laughed her deep belly laugh, which I loved. Momma smiled. At that exact moment, the phone rang. We all looked at each other with relief. "Dr. Lafferty," we shouted.

The good doctor always came through, maybe at the last minute, but he never disappointed us. I considered how convenient it was to suffer an affliction when my classes were at home—being homeschooled sure made life easier.

Momma did her usual, "Um, okay. Um, I see. Well, I don't know. Um—"Josey and I looked at each other in frustration.

Finally, Momma ended the call and turned to us. "Okay, you do have anemia, Caroline. Not a particularly severe case but enough to wear you down. We need to make some changes to your diet. You have to eat something besides grilled cheese sandwiches fried in heavy butter." She smiled.

"That's it? That's all he said? After all this time of us waitin' on pins and needles, that's all that old doctor could suggest?" Josey sent Momma and me each an incredulous look.

"Well, um, he did explain that childhood anemia is the result of a reduced number of red blood cells in the body. Caroline needs vitamins and supplements; plus, we have to be sure that she adds red meat, egg yolks, potatoes, tomatoes, beans, molasses, and raisins to her diet. It's important to encourage her to eat more citrus because Vitamin C will help her body absorb iron, which she needs.

"The doctor is phoning in a couple of prescriptions, but Caroline, if you don't want to swallow pills, you have to change the way you eat. I think we should cut grilled cheese sandwiches from your diet until you begin to eat better." Her eyes moved from my face to Josey's.

I moaned. Momma explained that she too suffered from childhood anemia, so maybe I had inherited it from her. I looked at Momma in an entirely different light after this revelation. I had never considered my mom as a child. I began to whine and protest, which they surely expected of me.

Now, I left their voices behind as forest sounds filled the ice-cold room. My head hurt so badly. *Is this worse than the hangover headache I experienced all those years ago?* I wanted to smile at that memory but had given up smiling hours earlier.

Instead, I was transported once more to my hotel room at Bunchrew. Still no husband in sight, so I had phoned room service.

"Hello, Ms. Caroline, it's Duncan. What can I do for you?"

"Duncan, don't you ever sleep? You waited on our table until late last night. Are you the only employee in this huge hotel?"

His happy laughter greeted me, and I pictured his head-to-toe blush. As always, when I thought about red hair and fair skin, I imagined Max. It was difficult for me not to miss him and Elizabeth. We had been inseparable for so long back home in Charleston.

Looking forward to the snack I had ordered, I read through some of the pamphlets lying on the table by the window. My entire body ached. I lowered myself into the comfy, plump window seat cushions upholstered in gold and green sprinkled with touches of red.

As I read about the Battle of Culloden, a gentle knock at the door aroused my hunger. I slowly approached the door as I continued to lean to the right. *When does a hangover pass?* During my life, I couldn't recall ever drinking so much.

"That's the last time!" I shouted as I opened the door.

"What? What's the last time? You okay, Ms. Caroline?" The boy's bright smile didn't look appropriate.

Duncan held a silver tray with a pot of tea and a slice of seed cake. That was the only thing I felt I might keep down. He looked handsome this morning, wearing a dark blue jacket and blue and gold tartan slacks. He stood in the hall, waiting for me to motion him inside.

"Oh, nothing, Duncan, I talk to myself." He brushed past and hurried toward the table by the window.

"You suffer from a hangover? Yeah, they're pretty nasty." He looked at me with sympathy.

"How old are you, Duncan? What can you possibly know about hangovers?"

He blushed as he set the pot of English Breakfast tea and a slice of seed cake gently before me. "You didn't specify the blend of tea you wanted, so I brought you my mom's favorite. Since you are such a big drinker, would you prefer your cake with a little whisky? We have several from which you can choose." He smiled innocently.

"You think I'm a big drinker?" I was flabbergasted by his remark.

He nodded. "Sure do, since every time I've seen you and Mr. Reid, you were drinking." His grand smile annoyed me.

"Listen, Duncan; we are not boozers. You know? Back in Charleston, we seldom drank at all. Well, not this much." I didn't need a youngster pointing out my faults. The pain I was enduring seemed penance enough for my earlier sins.

Hurriedly, the young man assured me that he forgave me for being a "lush." He explained that in Scotland, it was common. I groaned as I held my head. He didn't leave but kept looking at the empty chair beside me; I motioned for him to sit. That wasn't what I wanted. All I desired was to eat a few bites and crawl back to bed. I offered him a cup of tea.

"Oh, I can't. I'm working, ya know."

It seemed a little strange that he would sit down with me, but what the heck. *What do I know about the rules in Scotland?* I broke off a bite of the seed cake and nibbled. It was delicious.

"Wow, this cake is over the top! It's the best I've ever eaten."

"Great, I'll tell the baker. It was my mom, ya know."

With great pride, he explained that his family had worked for the lodge all their lives. He never attended college but gladly stayed here as had previous generations. "I hope to become a manager someday, ya know."

It was difficult not to like him. He was young and innocent. I devoured the cake and the delicious tea made by a Scottish company. Young Duncan recited many interesting facts about Inverness. With great emotion, he detailed the Battle of Culloden. Lovingly, the Scottish lad described many of his ancestors who died there. He appeared knowledgeable and created a strong desire to visit the site, which I figured Thom, and I would do today until Malcolm stole him away, and a hangover took my energy.

"Do you know him? Malcolm?" Duncan stood while explaining that Malcolm owned an extensive estate a few miles away.

"You should see it. Malcolm's place is gorgeous." He said that each year Malcolm hosted a massive party for the region. "Maybe, he'll invite ya since ye'll be a part of us soon, ya know?"

Before leaving, he enlightened me that Thom and Malcolm had shared a proper English breakfast before beginning their search for available property. "Yeah, yer husband and Malcolm seemed to hit it off really well. Mr. Reid sure looked happy to be with Mr. Dargie. I think they'll be great friends."

Duncan locked the door behind himself as he rushed away. His last comments sounded strange. *What did he mean that Thomas looked so happy with Malcolm? Does he not seem pleased with me?* The young man's words confused and alarmed me a little. *Have I demanded too much of Thom's time of late? Perhaps, he does seek the camaraderie of a man.* Duncan's words had created a sense of guilt that maybe I demanded too much from Thom. My husband was entitled to be happy and not tied to his needy wife. While I considered these things, there was another gentle knock on our door. Hesitantly, I opened it.

Duncan smiled. "Ms. Caroline, I want you to know that tomorrow's my day off. If Mr. Dargie and your husband have plans, it would please me to escort you to the old battlefield. We could make a day of it and enjoy lunch." He eagerly stared at me.

Still feeling a little confused by his previous statements, I agreed, and before I could reconsider my words, he was gone. "Oh, well, Thomas would enjoy another day with a male friend. He must miss Max." Slowly, I closed the door.

Chapter Thirteen

After eating every bite of the cake, I carried my cup of tea to the bedside table and stretched out in my bed of luxury. Outside the window, a gentle spring rain fell on this early, almost-summer day. Summer in Scotland runs from June 20 until September 22. We had arrived at the perfect time. Before long, the effects of the tea quieted the ravages of the alcohol from the previous evening. I fell deeply asleep.

Before long, treasured thoughts of Cape San Blas, Florida, arrived in my weary mind. I had ignored this other place that I loved—a dear place where so many pieces of my past hung gently in the dense, salty wind. *How could I forget to honor this place when thoughts of her come to me in quiet times?*

Cape San Blas, Florida, the thought of her always produced a smile. A tiny thread connected this small peninsula of land that extended westward from the mainland of Florida. It's located near the small town of Port St. Joe along Florida's Panhandle on the Emerald Coast. Our unique home situated on the Gulf of Mexico reflected dark green waters, which soothed our very souls upon every arrival. Miles of soft, smooth white sand cradled our steps as it protectively edged an aquatic preserve. The state park, located at the northern end, had won many awards. Each fall served as a shrine to the migrating Monarch butterfly as the beloved site also provided a home to nesting sea turtles; what more could any nature lover desire?

Early in her history, Cape San Blas was home to a confederate salt works until 1862 when this was halted by a landing party from the Union ship, the USS Kingfisher. *Yes, our homes on Cape San Blas, as much as the other two places we loved, surely held our secrets suspended in her salty air.*

When our parents decided to purchase beach homes on Cape San Blas, I thought it was too good to be true. Charleston had everything except great beaches. *How can one little girl live in paradise only to be given another slice?* Our families house-hunted together for months. The only thing Thom and I requested was that our new houses be situated close to each other, just like our Charleston places. Momma never explained why we needed two houses on the water but replied when asked, "Where else would we look for a second home, sugar? It must be near the water."

We received our wish for neighboring places when Momma came running into the hotel room so long ago, yelling for us to hurry. She and Mrs. Reid had found IT! "It" was the perfect beach cottage. She rushed us back to the site on Cape San Blas, where Jess Reid stood in the driveway with her arms crossed over her chest and a mean look on her face. I guessed she was discouraging anyone else from even thinking about looking at these homes.

Both places were gorgeous as they proudly stood on the shore side-by-side. One was a sunny yellow and the other a soft green. Our real estate agent waited with two contracts. The question became, which house went to whom? Momma whisked me inside each of the beauties. I was unable to decide. Finally, Thom took my hand. He led me outside. Deep in the back yard of the yellow one, behind a gigantic group of palm trees, stood a small house. It was a separate little structure.

We couldn't figure what the builder intended, but Thom sheepishly smiled as he whispered, "Don't girls love playhouses? Wouldn't this be perfect for you? We can meet here and share secrets. You should ask for this one."

That particular moment happened in our fourth school year together. We ran back to the house next door just as Momma and Daddy were signing the contract for the green one.

"Momma, you've got to stop! I want the yellow one. Thom wants this green house!"

The real estate agent stood in front of me. She was a large woman with rings of sweat under her arms. If there was ever a bully, she was it. "You're too late, honey. Your Mom selected this one, so Mrs. Reid is next door in her new place. Don't worry; you can visit the yellow house whenever you want. I'm sure no one will mind, dear."

I'm not a crybaby, but I began to wail, which I seldom did unless I felt ill. Momma looked at me sadly as I explained about the playhouse in the other yard. "She didn't even show it to us! Thom found it. Why should he and Max have a playhouse in their yard? They'll never use it." I pointed at the grumpy woman standing before me while accusing her of being a lousy agent. She attempted to smile, but what I received was a scowl.

The sourly disposed woman nudged me gently aside as she continued to explain it was "too late."

Daddy picked up the signed documents, held them in her face, and tore them into pieces. "You can write them again."

The Reid family rushed into the room, explaining they had made a mistake and wanted to purchase the green place. Thom and I hugged.

###

I had heard the door slowly open inside my hotel room. Then someone was on top of me. Fear washed over me as I recalled my experience in the pub. *Is Malcolm drunk and trying to kiss me again?* I smelled whisky; it was a familiar smell. There was also a whiff of Malcolm's cologne. It was difficult to open my eyes and let go of my pleasant dream of Cape San Blas. Relief flooded me when I raised my eyes to those of familiar chocolate.

It appeared almost twilight in the Bunchrew Hotel. "Thom, it's almost dark." I felt joy that it was him. "I've slept all day. I'd been feeling terrible from all the alcohol last night. Can we order room service and snuggle for the rest of the day?"

"Nil, Malcolm's waiting at Johnny Foxes for us, we need to hurry. He's a great guy. He'll be a good friend to us, Caroline. When ya get to know him, ye'll like him. Aye, I've forgiven him for the purple eye as I did Max when he punched me. Remember?" He patted me on the bottom and stretched out over the covers.

"Johnny Foxes? I don't know if I can. Do we have to go to such a noisy place? Ugh."

"What's wrong, Caroline?" He didn't sound happy, and he appeared tired.

Thoughts of the wrongs my husband endured at the hands of my Uncle Robert back in Charleston, added to the fact that he missed his brother, prompted me to hurry into the shower. As soon as I turned it on and felt the gush of hot water, I began to feel better—until a hand reached in and turned off the water.

"We don't have time, Caroline. Ye'll have to shower when we return. I told ya, Malcolm is waiting for us. He's an important man here. He can help us a great deal, plus he's fun. Come on. No one cares if you're a little smelly. You're always beautiful." He handed me a towel.

I took it with a laugh. "Hey, husband, do you remember that time at Cape San Blas when everyone complained about the way I smelled?"

My earlier dream still floated in my brain. I quickly brushed my hair, and we ran from the room. On the way, I told Thom one of my earlier thoughts.

I had turned to look at my boyfriend, gazing proudly at our day's work, our first sandcastle. It was beautiful. Finally, Thom looked at me. His look was not one of gratitude or admiration. He appeared shocked. "Um, Caroline, you should probably go get a shower. What happened to your hair?"

"Whew, Caroline Emma Corbett, you stink!"

Those kind words came from the pretty girl who reminded me of a miniature, Dolly Parton, with a "nice set," as the Reid brothers had earlier described Elizabeth Eisenhour. She had stood before me on that sweltering day looking absolutely perfect. Not even a hair on her raven head appeared out of place. A whiff of her caused me to bow my head. *Is that Shalimar?*

"Caroline, honey, you do smell. Why don't you run on inside and get cleaned up? I'll help young Mr. Reid here gather your things."

I felt the sting, not of another insect bite, but of tears that were welling up from deep inside. My daddy had kneeled in the sand, collecting my things beside Thom.

"Caroline, I know that you refuse to use deodorant because of the article you read about the possible link with cancer. But, honey, I don't think that was ever proven. You might want to consider using it in this heat. You look awful, darling."

Momma had now joined Daddy and the crowd and stood before me, also shining with that look of perfection. Of course, none of them had sat in the sun all day in the hot sand.

What I then heard from her was, "Look at you, Elizabeth. You are the perfect Southern belle. Honey, you take my breath away." Once, I had taken Momma's breath away. With my newly acquired body odor that everyone seemed intent on pointing out, before each other and the man I hoped to marry, I guessed also I took their breath away but not in a good way. *Couldn't someone have kindly taken me aside and pointed out my problem? Yes, I refuse to wear deodorant. I would take my chances with B.O., instead of the deadly C-word.* In later years, I would learn that I suffered from social anxiety, which can cause my problem. It seemed that if my self-confidence or esteem was threatened, that was the result.

So, there I stood before a resplendent sand construction that would win any competition. My body ached, I did stink, and I was humiliated by all those I must face for the rest of my life. Not knowing what else to do, I limped away to the pleasantries of my shower, where I cried.

Thom can't possibly love me after this. Indeed, he realizes the folly of his previous affections. Right now, he must regret ever swearing his love for me. Momma and Daddy must love me even though I might be a stinking, ugly mess. Max? Well, he has the perfect Elizabeth who strongly resembles Dolly.

I will return to the arms of Josey. She'll love me! Her love is unconditional. Always, there is Josey.

Chapter Fourteen

My eyes opened in the here and now without prompting. The pretty blue pot of flowers with their little pink-purple heads no longer appeared lovely. They were dead.

I groaned, "Not this again, God. Please call me home. I can't take much more! How long has it been? Will it never end?"

The feel of warm urine no longer upset me. Instead, it brought me peace with a moment of warmth. I no longer foolishly cried at my humiliation.

I had lost any pretense of entitlement because uncontrollable body functions stripped away those feelings. It was God and me against whoever it was that meant to kill me. My mind raced as though I might stop what waited if I could only figure out my life. There was a fight, a brawl, happening in my mind.

"Breathe deeply, Caroline. You must see this through. Who has done this to you?" My voice sounded like a whisper.

Silently I waited a few moments and watched the door. I was sure no one was at Alladale, except me, Caroline Emma Corbett Reid. I cried as the thought of the earlier lights which had flashed in the room came to my mind. *What was that, and why has no one arrived? Maybe, this will end sooner than I earlier thought.* Still, there had been no additional flashes or sounds. *Is someone laughing out in the hall? Did they smell the ammonia from my urine? Who is playing this sick game?*

As if to soothe me, the memories returned to Cape San Blas just before we left for Scotland. *Will I die when my dreams finally reach this place where I now exist, the here and now?*

When I entered my shiny white marble shower on that day of humiliation, I had kicked my swimsuit across the floor. A trail of sand followed in a long, messy line. I didn't care. It exhausted me to think of how hard I tried to please everyone and keep them all happy. Those I loved, except dear Josey, "Had thrown me under the bus." That was a phrase Josey used frequently. I stood in my new shower with its extensive rain system and let the water pound me. Daddy and Momma had probably discussed my body odor and decided that I needed a giant shower head to curb my potent stench.

The force of the water caused my face to sting from the excessive heat and biting insects of my and Thomas's earlier day on the beach. And my poor chest suffered what appeared to be first-degree burns, at least to me. My legs looked less like marshmallows and more like lightly broiled meat. The mousy brown hair that topped my head was heavily laced with sand. The finishing touch? Snot ran in strings from my nose. Indeed, I am a mess.

Angrily, I heavily pumped green tea shampoo into my hands and washed both my face and hair with it. The gentle fragrance soothed me, but I couldn't stop crying. The only thought that made my tears ease was Josey. *I must get home to her.* She would know how to handle these people who claimed to love me but constantly embarrassed and humiliated me. *Did they all have to point out my flaws in front of my boyfriend? He must regret ever promising to love me forever. Earlier, Max wouldn't even look at me. Why should he, when the lovely Southern belle, Elizabeth Eisenhour, stood by his side?* Poor Thom, I was all he had. Even my parents had demeaned me.

My eyes opened without prompting, and the thought of Josey jolted me to the present inside my chamber of horrors. I felt confident that I wouldn't be alive much longer. Delusions continued to assail me.

"I see you. Look at ya floating over me, my dearest Josey. I knew you would come. You've always been there when I needed you. Please, help me!"

The shackles no longer hurt. I was past feeling as I attempted to reach toward Josey, who, for some reason, hung in the air. Nothing mattered anymore, but the remembrances kept coming. *How much longer can I last?*

Back in Florida, I had decided that running away to catch a bus back to Charleston might not be a good idea since there weren't any on the Cape. In that case, I would refuse to speak ever again. For the remainder of my days, I, Caroline Emma Corbett, would be mute. *That will serve them right. No, they will not make me use deodorant just as they couldn't stop my eating cheese sandwiches fried in butter. When they all succumb to cancer, I might stink, but I will not endanger myself to please them. Also, I will set Thom free from his commitment to me.*

After reaching such hallmark decisions, I smiled. For the first time in my life, I braided my long locks. That was something Momma always did, but I would never let her do it again. I would punish them all, including Momma, for the rest of their miserable existence. The outcome of my first braid was not perfect, but like me, it was passable. A pretty little turquoise sundress hung in my closet. It was brand-new; I tied a matching satin bow at the end of my braid. Traipsing into Momma's room, I found her treasured pink Lancôme lipstick and applied it sparingly. *I look stunning.*

When I walked out to the pool, everyone was in it, laughing and throwing water at each other. *Everyone looks so lame!* I had thought. The Southern belle, miniature Dolly, now appeared a mess. Her perfect shadowy hair hung limply in her eyes. Max was sunburned pretty severely; he wasn't a pretty sight. Momma, even she, had fallen prey to the insects and heat. Mr. and Mrs. Reid also looked ghastly. Only Thom shined with his deep tan and chocolate eyes. *How can he always remain pristine?* None of them mattered to me now.

With my head high, I sauntered past them with one of Momma's glossy magazines and sat in the shade at the back. Everyone became ghostly quiet; I refused to look at them. Their earlier boisterous racket died. Not saying a word, I rose from my recliner and hastened to the kitchen. When I returned, without a word, I stopped in front of them and took a large sip of iced pink lemonade. It felt soothing. The cold of the ice soothed my parched throat. Walking as my Momma did, like a queen, I strode to my earlier seat.

"Wow, honey, you look so pretty."

I ignored Daddy's phony compliment. Earlier, he showed his true colors. Oh, how I longed to shout, "I no longer smell, but all of you might want to consider a shower!" *Maybe everyone has body odor, and it doesn't affect just me?* Instead of reacting to them, I ignored them and stared at my magazine until I realized that I was holding it upside down. Quickly, I adjusted it with my head glued to an ad for—I couldn't believe it—a deodorant. I almost laughed.

"Hey, Caroline, that lemonade looks great. Got an extra glass?" Max's soft words failed to impress me.

If only he could see how ridiculous he looks, like a lobster. Without a word, I turned my page away from the interesting ad for a deodorant to one for lipstick. My eyes refused to leave the bronzed goddess's page, who smiled with lips that looked two times larger than most. It was a shame that none of the earlier insects hadn't assaulted my lips. Maybe they would have swollen like that poor woman's lips.

My actions soon emptied the pool. Everyone hurried away like scurrying ants; I hoped to their showers as I realized *I'm not the only one who smells bad.* The only one remaining was Thom. He hadn't hurt me, but I was freeing him from the likes of me to find a worthy wife—one who wouldn't stink and look a mess. I thought of Paula Peterson, his first love, who had been without flaws.

"Caroline Emma, you okay? You're acting very strange. You mad at me?" The blond boy's innocence touched me.

At that moment, I decided to give myself latitude in my quest never to speak again. "Nope, I'm not mad at you, but I'm freeing you, Thomas. You deserve better than me. You need someone who will never stink or look bad. Since I'm not that person, you're free to pursue anyone you like. That is, except for Paula Peterson, who is in Heaven with Jesus. She's taken." I bowed my head.

When I looked into his coffee-colored eyes a minute later, I was shocked to see tears, not a copious amount but a gentle mist.

He took my hand. "Don't you ever say that again. You're my girl, Caroline. No one is more perfect for me. I want you to know that I understood how hard it was for you to sit beside me today in that buggy, hot place in the sand. You didn't complain, not once, even when I almost walked away from my project because of the pain that I experienced from the bugs and heat. For the rest of my life, I'll never doubt your commitment."

Those thoughts turned me now to a more current time here in Scotland.

Thom was driving us to Johnny Foxes after spending the day with Malcolm instead of me. Without warning, he turned off onto the side of the road. Grasping my head with both hands, he kissed me with such passion that I had trouble breathing.

"Don't you ever forget how much I love you, Caroline. I miss Max and Dad so much. I know that you experience the same feelings. I've ignored you today, and I don't know why. Please, forgive me. Can you? It's just that I starve for the friendships I left behind. You and I have been together so much these past weeks. It's not that I tire of you. Can you understand this, because I'm not taking away much from my own words?" His blond head bowed with emotion.

My earlier conversation with Duncan had proven helpful in how I should respond. The young lad had prepared me for something like this. *How can one as young as Duncan be that wise?*

"Of course, I understand completely. That's why I planned my day tomorrow with Duncan. We're going to visit the site of the infamous Battle of Culloden. You can plan another day with Malcolm. Thomas, you deserve this. You see, I want you to be happy. Duncan is a great deal of fun and a rather impressive historian. I'll pass on to you everything that I learn tomorrow."

"My goodness, Caroline, I don't know what to say except that it seems Scotland is Aontaithe. I love you."

When we entered Johnny Foxes, the music played, and the whisky flowed. Malcolm stood at the center of the bar, surrounded by locals. When we walked into the room, they all cheered as though we were old friends, and they were welcoming us home. *Maybe, we are all connected from a previous life and feel a bond that we can't explain?*

"What'll it be, lassie?"

"A whisky, please."

"Malcolm? Duncan? Where are ye? How long have I been here? Aren't you searching for me?" Only a smelly, cold room answered.

Chapter Fifteen

The Battle of Culloden was the last pitched battle ever to be waged on British soil. The Jacobite army of Sir Edward Stuart wanted to consolidate their power over Scotland. The soldiers were able to obtain some support from the French government in their bloody attempt as early as 1745. By 1746, they faced William Augustus, Duke of Cumberland, and his forces on Drumossie Moor in the Scottish Highlands. The terrain there gave Cumberland's well-rested men the edge. The Jacobites had suffered for so long and were exhausted on the day of battle. The brave warriors lost the fight. Somewhere between 1,500 and 2,000, men were severely wounded or died in a struggle that lasted a little over an hour. Only about 300 government soldiers were killed or injured. Cumberland's brutal attacks, on the remaining Jacobites and their sympathizers, earned him the title "Butcher." After this battle, the British tried to undermine the Scottish clan system from which most of the uprisings came. The government forces carried out their attacks for years.

The National Trust for Scotland lovingly maintained the site. Today, I stood beside Duncan, shoulder-to-shoulder, as he described in detail the bloody battle. It was a particularly chilly morning for June. We stood together in the misty early morning light. I felt a shiver as I stared at a place where so many men died.

"I'm not even from here, but I can feel something powerful. It's almost as if I hear them crying from the earth that mixed with their blood."

"Aye, I as well. I always experience this same feeling. Ya have a great deal of compassion, Caroline." His brown eyes looked intently into my dark ones. We had developed a deep friendship, which he admitted to me. I thought he was so sweet.

"What time do Malcolm and Thomas want us to join them tonight at Johnny Foxes?"

Duncan looked off into the distance. "Well, they said at five, but I have a feeling we could show up an hour early and find them leaning on the bar."

I didn't discuss it with Thomas, but lately, I was worried about all of the drinking we had done since arriving in Scotland. Early this morning, after he and Malcolm left the room, I kneeled and prayed for guidance. There was a link to alcoholism in both the Corbett and Reid families. I had never consumed much alcohol, but as of late, that had changed. *Is it because I am away from home and the cautious eyes of my family and town, in a new place that gives me a sense of freedom?* Earlier in the morning, Duncan's words as he described me as a "boozer" hadn't helped.

"Duncan, is there a Methodist Church close? I believe my husband and I need to become part of a church family. We always attended back in the US. We need a group to hold us responsible."

"Aye, the Methodist Church is located near, I'll show ya on the way home." The look he gave me said that he understood.

We spent the rest of the day at the Inverness Museum and Art Gallery. A light lunch at a local pub suited both of us. I was thankful for Duncan's friendship; he seemed to know many people and was well-liked. Together, we shared common interests and spent a lot of time laughing. Duncan was young, but once I understood him, he was knowledgeable.

"Aye, I could have gone to college. Some of my family did, but most didn't, ya know?" The similarities between Max and Duncan rose again in my mind, not only the flaming red hair but also the fair skin, brown eyes, and the hysterically witty sense of humor.

"I always knew what I wanted to do with me time. I'd be thrilled as the Manager of the hotel. That's why I work in every department. If I understand everything, maybe they'll see me as worthy someday."

"I admire you, Duncan. Many of my friends back in the States spent a fortune for a college education, only to end up not using it or working in a different field for which they didn't train. I'd say you're blessed knowing what you want so early. It all makes sense to me.

"By the way, I needed this time away from Thomas, or maybe I should say that you were right earlier. He might need some time with other men away from me. He misses his brother, Max. You remind us very much of him."

Duncan's dark eyes blazed as he asked me to describe the older brother. We left the pub to drive back to the hotel, where I immediately went to the room for a quick nap before meeting Malcolm and Thomas for dinner. Duncan went to work at the front desk. What he didn't say, but we discovered later, was that our young lad hailed from a wealthy Scottish family. He was related to the owners of the inn.

When I entered the room, drawn shades greeted me. I knew that I had not left them that way. As I slipped gently into bed, a figure turned to face me. It was Thom.

"Where have ya been?" He looked tired.

In great detail, I outlined my day and the fun that Duncan and I shared. He listened intently to my story.

"Did ya have anything to drink?"

I was puzzled. "Aye, a cup of tea, why?"

Thomas took a deep breath. "Well, I've been concerned with yer drinking lately, Caroline. Ya worry me. We both know there's a link to alcoholism in our families, so we must use caution. Plus, we need to find a Methodist church. I guess they have them."

"Yes, they do. I know where one is located."

Thom hugged me. "Malcolm would like to join us on Sunday. He's a little concerned about his drinking. I guess we all have skeletons in our closets."

"Aye, we're all so much alike, aren't we? I'm glad that we're here in 'Alba.'"

A heavy snore met my words. In the past, Duncan had referred to his native land as "Alba."

"So, what skeletons do ya hold for us, Alba? Aye, I'm soon to become one, I guess." My words sounded hollow and sad.

Chapter Sixteen

"Yes, what secrets do you hold, Scotland? Was the plan always that Thom and I should die here? So, is it night again? Is this the second one or the third or more? Does it matter?"

Outside, all sorts of night animals made their calls.

Was that a wolf? No, I remembered that wolves became extinct in Scotland, thanks to Sir Ewen Cameron, in 1680, although rumors swirled of sightings as late as the eighteenth century and one reported as late as 1888.

"Oh, Thomas, you and your dreams, how you longed to create a controlled wolf reserve in your beloved land. Did too many locals object? Perhaps, they didn't understand your desire for ecological balance as Scotland once demonstrated before the rape of the land began in the name of progress? How I wish that you lay beside me tonight. Together, we would imagine the cry of the wild."

What is that I hear? Is it maybe a coyote? No, now, I recall that they were hunted to extinction in both England and Wales. Unless I'm living in the fifteenth century then, no, that cry is not a coyote. Well, what is it?

I heard a rustle on my windowsill. Straining with fear to discover what had entered the room, I shivered at the sight of a tawny owl. "Ah, you've returned? At least, someone cares about me."

Didn't an owl come earlier? No, maybe it was another bird? Was it a sparrow? Confusion controlled my mind. *How long have I been here?* I hadn't a clue. *Is this the second night or the third? If this is the third, my life on earth is almost at an end.* I laughed. I realized that I must be mad.

The little owl was about the size of a pigeon with a rounded body and head. A ring of dark feathers surrounded his circular face and large dark eyes. I had never been so close to one. Maybe he realized that I wasn't a threat, or did he know I was almost dead? His little body was a reddish-brown with a paler color underneath. He didn't make a sound. He simply sat on the sill and stared at me. The look that he gave me seemed sad. I was so starved for companionship that I attempted to reach toward him. Of course, I was unable. My little friend stayed only a short time before he flew away. I cried at his departure.

"Please, come again. I'm so lonely."

Extreme weakness washed over me. I was aware that I would be unable to walk from this bed if I was ever freed. I fell back into my previous reverie.

Duncan had requested to drive us to Malcolm's estate for dinner. The four of us had enjoyed Johnny Foxes so much that Malcolm had invited our young friend to join us for the meal.

The handsome lad never ceased to amaze me, like when he picked us up in this four-seater Aston Martin Rapide S. He explained as he drove that his family owned a part of the hotel. It all made sense now. The young man is not only handsome but humble and very wealthy.

"Wait 'til ya see this house. I mean, ya won't believe his place. It's gorgeous."

While he raved about Malcolm's home, I thought that this kid was doing all right for himself. Slowly, to maximize the WOW effect of Malcolm's gorgeous home, Duncan became deathly quiet, which was unusual for him, as we drew closer.

The extensive gravel sweep of the entrance led up a graceful incline to the top of a small hill where the majestic Georgian-designed home stood shining like a stately castle. It was that, indeed. The exterior was block construction with a harling surface and decorative quoins. The home featured a Venetian window above the front door, ashlar quoins, a stringcourse, and pitched dormer windows in the hipped Mansard roof.

The main entrance was in the eastern facade, which allowed guests access to the front door. All of this elegance stood under a black Welsh slate roof with traditional cast-iron rainwater goods. The entire estate stood upon over five hundred and thirty acres; the extensive gardens and lawn thrilled me as I remembered the wedding-cake abode and the gold home of Thomas and my childhoods.

The butler, Charles, didn't smile but politely invited us inside. This large man later became a friend of ours, but at our first meeting, he was reserved, at least until further in the evening. Charles dressed in chinos and a white oxford shirt. The creases in his trousers were straight as arrows. His shoes were polished to a "spit shine," as we say in America. Apparently, he was well-schooled for his vocation.

I wished that Duncan would be quiet so I could hear what Charles said, but the young lad appeared very nervous and excited. I had seen him this way before, and he would constantly talk, which he did on that night long ago. Traditional Scottish music played softly in the background. We were seated and offered drinks. While we waited for our host, I studied every detail I could to help Thom in our new home's design process. Eagerly, I turned to take stock of the large entrance hall we had passed earlier. It led into a reception room that featured a galleried landing, which I guessed could serve as a dining space for larger parties.

We sipped whisky. Charles served a platter of hors d' oeuvres. I smiled at my husband as I imagined our grander home, where we would host large parties. Inside Malcolm's lavish mansion, the drawing-room projected a bright, light, and airy feeling. The colors of the room were pulled from a giant, thick rug which featured golds, blues, and reds. With the inviting ambiance, we began to relax with the whisky and soft music.

After a brief wait, Malcolm strode into the room. He dressed in a dark kilt with a jacket that matched. His lightly tanned skin attested to the fact that this Scot loved the outdoors. His kindness and graciousness to us surprised me because I realized he must be busy. Our friend was a large man with copper-red hair. The late-evening light shone upon it through a partially open window. He appeared majestic with his large brown eyes and a ruddy complexion. I thought that he must have been a great athlete at one time, with his broad shoulders and trim waist. I estimated his age at about fifty.

Does he have a wife? I never heard mention of one. Just as I decided to ask, a gorgeous woman delicately entered. Her steps were so nimble that I didn't hear a sound.

Molly stood before us with a sweet smile. She appeared friendly and sunny with long red hair and the fairest of skin. From her complexion, the young woman never had sat in the sunshine. The dress she wore was a sheer rose color. I could see through it. It reminded me of Mrs. Reid's nightgown when I climbed into her bed upon the death of Paula Peterson. Molly's flair for matching the unusual impressed me. The dark lipstick she wore looked stunning. I would never have thought that color would work on a redhead, but it did.

Malcolm introduced her as his fiancée. She was from Ireland. When she spoke, her voice was sweet and soft and lilting. It was apparent to me that we would become good friends. She and I walked to one of the large open windows where we looked down on a pristine lake that was as smooth as silk. The lawn and gardens were immaculate with the greenest of grass, and I knew that Mrs. Reid would have loved to see all of the bright, bold flowers. She would have identified each shrub, tree, and bloom. Although I couldn't do that, I could appreciate the stunning effect.

Molly explained that in her earlier years, she did a little modeling. She had that look. Later, Malcolm revealed the lovely young woman had been quite famous. Now, she owned a boutique in Inverness. The more we talked, the better I liked her. It felt as if I had made a lasting friend, even though we had just met. When

Charles announced dinner, we didn't move. He had to call us a second time. As we laughingly walked into the dining room, I hadn't felt such peace since leaving Charleston.

After we were seated, the laughter and small talk continued long into the night. At one point, I blurted out an embarrassing statement. "Oh, Thomas, it's as if we have Max and Elizabeth here with us. Doesn't Molly remind you of our Elizabeth?"

Everything grew quiet. Duncan looked at me with a startled look because Thom obviously disagreed. He lowered his head and shook it.

Suddenly, he appeared confused. "I don't see it, Caroline. Molly looks nothing like Elizabeth. I mean, they're both gorgeous women, but Liz has raven hair and big, um, you know." He held his cupped hands to his chest to emphasize Elizabeth's ample bosom. I remembered I had once labeled her as a miniature, Dolly Parton. Molly blushed, and so did Duncan.

"No, I mean, yes, Elizabeth does, but there's a spirit about Molly that makes me feel loved like my sister-in-law makes me feel."

Everyone laughed, but my husband just couldn't let it rest. Sometimes, when Thomas attempted to make a point, he would do this. "You know what I mean. Molly, well, she's a little lassie." He smiled as everyone lowered their heads.

All of this banter caused a memory to pop into my mind, which I had to share. When I turned thirteen, it was the same time that Max and Elizabeth threw a big party to celebrate a milestone in their relationship. Max had both their names inscribed inside a heart that hung on a sterling silver bracelet. It was exquisite. The young couple glowed as they gazed into each other's eyes; I had felt a little jealous. Elizabeth always seemed to have everything.

To make me feel better, Momma gave me an "I've got boobs" party. I feared that I might never have boobs because I was so tiny for all of my young life. That thought became an obsession and a joke among my family and friends, so my little party was hysterical. Just our small group, Thom and me, with Max and Elizabeth, celebrated with our parents in Charleston. Momma bought a cool cake from our favorite bakery, which proudly displayed "a large set." The cake was cute.

My set wasn't so pronounced, but I had turned into a charming Southern belle, if I may say. Elizabeth and I had become like sisters. The four of us were always together unless the two brothers had a sports event. In that case, Elizabeth and I were never far apart. I was unaware of how desperately I missed my friend. Now, maybe, Molly would be the sister I craved.

After I shared this experience, the subject turned to, what else, more boobs. We hadn't drunk much. I guessed we were aware that earlier we had expressed fear of becoming alcoholics. It was just that we were enjoying each other so much. I'll never forget Duncan's face. He threw his head back and laughed, shocked that we would focus on such a subject at dinner. Neither he nor Molly blushed any longer in our presence, probably because we embarrassed them so often. Everyone but Duncan had a boobs story.

I had to relay something else that happened after my childhood friend, Paula Peterson died.

Mr. Reid had walked toward me with a strange look. "Um, look here, Caroline, Mrs. Reid is in a bad way. Something's not right with her. Before I phone our doctor, I want to try one more thing. It involves you. You interested?" He looked hopeful, just like his sons, who surrounded me.

"Are you kidding? I'd do anything to help Mrs. Reid. At one time, I was her little girl. That is until Paula Peterson came along." I smiled as he nodded.

"Exactly, that's what I need you to do. Remind Mrs. Reid how important she is to you and that you want to be her little girl again. Can you do that?" Max and Thomas remained on each side of me.

"Okay. Sure, I can do that." Proudly, I strutted up the stairs. I felt needed.

They all accompanied me up the posh stairs, which sported thick Oriental rug runners. Mr. Reid stopped the boys and shook his head that they weren't to go with me. Alone, I stumbled into the dark, chilly room. I couldn't see it very well. Unlike most of the rest of the house, I had never been inside this space.

Quietly, I stood beside her bed, and I wondered how to begin. Hearing her soft moans caused my heart to break for her. *If I had died, would she be so sad? I questioned.* Not knowing what else to do, I climbed into her bed.

The thick duvet was heavy and cold. It felt lavish with dense embroidery and golden tassels sewed on the ends. I smelled a fragrance, which was just like the one Mrs. Reid always wore. I loved her perfume. Gently, I snuggled close to her back and held her. A feeling of peace settled over me. I softly squeezed her right arm like Thom did to comfort me. Her breathing was heavy and regular, accompanied by tiny groans. Before long, I also fell asleep beside her.

At some point, I felt her turn toward me. Her face was mere inches from mine. Her long blond hair cascaded over chocolate eyes. Usually, she wore her hair piled on the top of her head. With it down, she looked so young. A dark blue sleep mask was pulled back over her hair. She wore a long thin gown. I could see right through it and felt embarrassed, looking at her chest but couldn't help it. *So this is how boobs look?* I had thought. I sure wish I would grow some. As I continued to stare, she opened her brown eyes. A look of wonderment spread over her face.

"Paula, is that you?"

I hated to disappoint her. "No, ma'am, it's only me, Caroline Emma Corbett. Do you remember me?"

Her gentle laugh pleased me. *Maybe she's not as damaged as Mr. Reid thought earlier.*

"Yes, of course, I know who you are. For a moment, you looked like my Paula." She tousled my hair. Her words stung.

"No, ma'am, I'm not nearly as pretty as Paula Peterson. My Momma says she looked like an angel. My Daddy calls me a demon, so I'm not exactly pretty like her." I lowered my eyes as tears gently fell with the recollection of my dead friend.

"What's this? Whoever said that you aren't as pretty as Paula? Everyone knows that Caroline Emma Corbett is the queen of Charleston. Paula was pretty, but there's something about you, Caroline, that's more than pretty.

"You know that Thom will marry you, don't you? You are going to be my daughter-in-law someday, way in the future. I will be so pleased. Until that time, yes, you are my little girl. I'll never let anyone else claim that spot. I promise. Even with Paula, I especially loved you." Her news brightened my weary spirit.

Quickly, I confided the latest news. Max would now marry Elizabeth Eisenhour and change her last name to Reid. Thomas and I were on again in our wedding plans. She kissed me just like old times before Paula Peterson came into our lives.

"I miss Paula. She's the first one I think of now. Even before Max and Thom. When will I stop missing her, Mrs. Reid?"

My tears fell freely. Mrs. Reid's salty tears mingled with mine. I tasted them, wondering which were mine and which were hers? The thought of pricking our fingers to become blood sisters came to mind. Softly, I asked Mrs. Reid if the mingling of our tears created a similar bond.

"No, my darling, we are much more than that. You and I are like family. Now, I must get out of this bed and find the rest of my brood. We have an adventure waiting." Her face remained tired-looking but glowed with peace.

"I know about the beach cottages and plans to spend the summer there finally. Max told me. Don't be angry with him. I wish that Paula could have joined us. You know what? Her fussy parents won't let her have a funeral. They're going to bury her in a place we don't know. Thom's pretty upset, but I explained what Momma told me about ol' Sissy Smothers. Thom and I don't think she's a real person."

Mrs. Reid hugged me. "What? Ol' Sissy Smothers? Yes, she's a real person who's about a hundred years old. She lives to attend funerals. I won't be having one either. I never cared for them or her."

Mrs. Reid stood in front of me. I looked again through her nightgown at her chest. I wanted to ask her when I might expect my boobs, but I decided to wait for a better time.

I had expected the boisterous laughter to shower forth from my friends and fellow diners, but everyone became silent and lowered their heads. Even Thomas looked shaken.

"Wow, Caroline. I had forgotten about that. We were very young. You always stood up to the challenge. No wonder I love you so much."

The evening turned somber as we finished our dessert of Scottish Cranachan, which I had never tasted before. It was delicious. Charles set another helping in front of me. Only I received a second serving. His generous smile prompted the same from me.

"Miss Caroline, that was, indeed, such a sweet story. I am touched."

The broad smile from the butler warmed my heart. I had begun to think that he didn't like Thomas and me. Suddenly, everyone began sharing a sad tale from their early childhoods. We all had them.

As we met in the library facing the Northwest just before 10 p.m., a lovely sunset spread out before us. The sky appeared dark, but the low-lying clouds were fluffy white with streaks of pink and blue. The sight was almost eerie.

Charles froze when he saw it. He coughed and nearly choked. Losing control, he whispered, "This is how the sky looked the evening my wife died. I'll never forget. I haven't seen one like it since." He rushed from the room, brimming with emotion.

Molly and Malcolm looked shocked as they both quickly stood. "I've never heard Charles say anything to our guests except to ask perfunctory questions. This night is a first."

To clear the air and change the subject, Thomas and Malcolm began to talk about our new home. My husband hadn't told me that they had found the perfect site to build our dream castle earlier that day. Shock at their words made me lose my generous smile. I didn't know why Thom had failed to share such important information. Even Malcolm looked surprised that Thom forgot to mention the "perfect place to build." My husband seemed a little uneasy.

"What's this? You haven't taken me to this building site? From Malcolm's description, it sounds perfect. Why are you holding out?"

I hated to go back to the real world of problems. In the safe confidence of each other, the five of us had found an escape from all of life's challenges. It felt as if we could share anything. Even Duncan had shared several meaningful episodes in his young life. Thomas surprised me as he communicated his fear about building here.

"You see, I'm not licensed in Scotland. I know that I could probably design it and hire a builder to bring our dream to life, but, Caroline, a piece of me died back in Charleston when Uncle Robert spread those lies about me. It hurt when the people we loved believed falsehoods and turned against us. That experience left me never wanting to build again. I understand your disappointment, my darling. That's why I've avoided discussing it."

His words baffled me. *Well, this is excellent news. We moved to Scotland to build our sandcastle in the snow, but my builder husband is afraid to begin.*

My hands began to shake with his revelation. "What will we do?"

Malcolm pounded Thomas on the back. "You buy a property that closely meets your needs, and you are happy to find it. Then you move on with your lives in this land of eccentric people and sunsets that make you cry. It happens every day. I didn't build Taigh Dargie, ya know? No, she's an old lady with a lot of money poured into her, but she's worth every penny to us." He smiled at Molly as they both looked around their house.

His words made perfect sense. Of course, instead of suffering all the headaches that building a large home would bring, we would begin looking for something on the market. Not having to face all the decisions to complete our dream made the process feel more accessible. I loudly exhaled the breath I had been holding, and I smiled at my husband. The air between us finally cleared.

"This is great news. When do we begin looking?"

Thomas walked to me. "I've been afraid that ya would be upset with me. Ya can't imagine how relieved I am. After urging ye to come here with me promising to construct the perfect new home, how could I tell ya that I no longer wanted to create it? If we can find a breathtaking place that meets all our needs, how much simpler? Right? Are ya okay with this new idea?"

"I hate to point this out, but the possibility of finding the 'perfect' place that meets 'all yer needs' seldom happens. It's more like finding a place that ye can settle for and releasing all earlier expectations. Are ya prepared to compromise? It might be worth it to accept less house but keep more of yer sanity."

Duncan moved closer to us. "I've never been as happy as when I'm with ya four. Ya see, because I'm so much younger than all of ya, yer acceptance means the world to me. I feel a deep fondness for each of ye, aye, yer like my family. I've never before felt connected like the four of ya make me feel."

I knew what he meant. For the first time since leaving Charleston, I felt like my life had been given back to me. In the faces of these friends, I had found a new family. We turned back toward the sunset, but it was gone.

"Is there a sunset tonight?" I was unable to look, but I tried to recall if this was night number two or three. If it was three, tomorrow should be my end. This realization made me ecstatic that the torture was almost over.

Chapter Seventeen

Thomas and I set out early the next day to find our new home. Malcolm recommended us to an agent friend who had lived in Inverness all of his life.

"I think yer making a wise choice by looking for a home already built. This way, ya see, ya know what yer getting." The handsome Scottish agent smiled at me in the rearview mirror.

I thought for a moment. *Yes, and ye'll be receiving a hefty commission. Everybody wins!* I smiled back at him.

Our new approach still didn't feel quite right to me. We had always planned to build. I missed the excitement of watching my husband prepare and work for us, to make a home that we dreamed of together. *Can we possibly find one already completed that would please us?* I had my doubts.

So far, on our first day, we had visited four homes. Not one of them was right. Exhaustion had overtaken me, or was it disappointment? After looking for over five hours, we all agreed to call it a day and start early the next morning. The agent deposited us safely back at the hotel. We trudged back to our room.

"Okay, what's wrong, Caroline? I know something's bothering ya, ye've hardly spoken all afternoon."

After I explained that nothing he showed us even came close to my expectations, Thomas nodded. "Aye, it was a bit of a disappointment. Don't give up on it. Remember, he promised an auspicious day tomorrow. We'll find it."

After showering, we leisurely strolled into the dining room. There sat Malcolm and Molly in the back at our favorite table. "Just the couple we hoped to see. Come join us and tell us about yer first day at house-hunting." Many hugs and kisses helped to brighten my sagging spirits.

Duncan rushed to our table, excited. "Aye, I'd love to hear what ya saw and yer reactions. Did ya find the perfect place?"

Highly disappointed, I shook my head. Duncan hurried away. Our friend, I found, only liked to hear happy news. If it wasn't, he just rushed away. Malcolm and Molly offered encouragement that tomorrow was another day with a different set of houses.

The hours rolled past, and we talked until late. Seeing them perked me up. I felt encouraged by their boost of confidence.

After a good night's rest, we met the agent early the next morning to resume our hunt. At our instructions, the agent only had shown us properties that had already been refurbished and needed little work. Again, we returned home discouraged. My big dreams crashed as I thought of Charleston's wedding-cake home with all that room, which Daddy wouldn't use. *How can I tell Thom that I want to go back to the States and call off this madness?*

Once again, the next day, we searched for hours only to return disheartened. When we pulled up to the hotel, the agent turned to us. "I hate to be a spoiler, but there aren't any more homes to show ya right now. We can wait until another home is listed. There are a few properties that I know will come on the market next year. Are ya certain that none of today's pleased ye?" He looked as disappointed as I felt.

Thomas looked at me as if hoping I might reconsider one of them, but there wasn't one I would even mull over. I shook my head, no.

The agent nodded. "Well, ya did say going into this that ya wouldn't be in a hurry. We'll find it. Don't despair. It'll take a little longer, that's all." His sweet smile did little to lift the misery I felt. We had made a significant miscalculation.

The agent reiterated that as soon as he received word of another property, he would phone us. I almost closed the car door when he asked, "Are ya sure ye won't consider an estate that needs some work? Ye'll get a better price, and with your skills, Mr. Reid, ya might enjoy the renovation process. See, I have one home that checks most of yer boxes, but it needs a little work. Well, maybe, a lot of work, but she's a beauty. Her name is Alladale. The location's just where ya want. Would ye like to see her?"

Thom turned to me with fire in his coffee-colored eyes. "Aye, we would but not now. Let's do it tomorrow."

Mr. Wilson appeared disappointed but handed Thom two brochures about the new candidate. I felt that he already knew he had found the exact place of our dreams. *Maybe, he planned to show all the others first and save Alladale to the end so that we could truly appreciate it? Malcolm was correct; this guy is smooth.*

Once more, eagerness for tomorrow beckoned us to keep hope and not despair. We hurried to our room so that we could study the brochures about this new place. When we entered the room, Thom spread the first glossy pamphlet on the table by the window. I was afraid to look.

"Caroline, look at this! She's beautiful, this Alladale. Can you imagine 23,000 acres? We can plan our nature reserve and bring all the animals that we want. The house is stunning. I don't know how much work she needs, but look at this. Why didn't that agent show us this on the first day? We might already be preparing for the closing."

I walked to the table and gathered up the brochures—one pictured Alladale in the winter surrounded by snow. The building appeared almost yellow against the backdrop of white. It was the most beautiful house I had ever seen.

The other showed her on a summer day. In that photo, against the dark green grass and shrubs, she appeared beige with a dark blue roof. It looked like two different structures. My heart thumped as I looked at what I knew would become our new home.

This place, called Alladale, was truly magnificent. She was everything I had dreamed of locating. The site was picture-perfect, proudly beckoning to us from the forest of North Scotland. Those Scot pines in the pictures were direct descendants of the first pines to arrive in Scotland after the Late Glacial Period. This home that stood surrounded by descendants of the Caledonian forest would be ours. The trees alone beckoned me.

After a long, hot shower, we entered the dining room. Unfortunately, no friends waited for us now that we had something to share. We pondered the information.

Duncan hurried over. "Did ya find it?"

"Aye, maybe, lad, did ya ever hear of Alladale?"

Duncan smiled and didn't appear surprised. "Aye, of course, just one of the most desirable places in Scotland. Mr. Wilson knew as soon as he met ya that it was the perfect place for ya, but he had to make sure that ye knew it. He's a great agent."

I found those words incredulous. Everyone seemed to know we would love Alladale, but the agent had waited. "I wish he would've shown her to us first. Why didn't he?"

Thom reminded me that early on, we had requested a place that didn't need much work. Now that he saw this beauty, he'd changed his mind. We could hardly wait for the next day. My husband even considered phoning Mr. Wilson to request we see it that night, but that didn't seem fair to the agent, so we agreed to wait.

All evening, we studied the data. Thom pointed out that in the main house or lodge, we could fashion seven double en suite rooms. He continued that deeper into the forest, another building named Deanich could house a group of up to sixteen guests. I couldn't believe our good fortune. This possibility was bigger than our dream. He surprised me by adding that he would like to add two new cottages of his own design.

I was further excited when I realized that by doing this, Thom's earlier desire to create a new house would be fulfilled. Everything was falling into place. In my heart, I knew we had found our Scottish dream.

We were unable to sleep. When I finally dozed off, my husband would wake me with new ideas or questions that caused us to rush back to the pamphlets waiting on the window table. Early the next morning, we waited for Mr. Wilson, filled with a yearning to discover this magical place called Alladale. As if he knew we were waiting, Mr. Wilson arrived earlier than we had discussed. His smile told me that he also knew our dreams were about to unfold before our eyes.

I questioned him in aggravation. "Why didn't ya show us this place first? We could already have made our offer, and maybe freed ourselves from this pressure to find a home."

With a knowing smile, Mr. Wilson replied, "Aye, I could have done that, but I wouldn't have been following yer instructions, now would I? I needed to exhaust all my options for ya to understand the value of what I'm about to show ye." With that, he swept us away to the enchanting land of Alladale.

I jumped awake in the bed. I felt as if I was in Mr. Wilson's car, and he had stopped suddenly. The room was dark and cold. My heart feared for Thom. *What end did he meet?* The fear that shook me remained for about an hour. By slowly adjusting my breathing, I was able to fall into unconsciousness or deep sleep. Whatever was happening to me, my body seemed to adapt and helped by removing me to a better time.

"I still love you, Alladale. Forever, you will hold a piece of my heart." My voice, now a mere whisper, floated on the cold wind from the open window.

Chapter Eighteen

Not a word passed as we drove to our future home; at least I hoped it was our next place. *Does Mr. Wilson go slowly on purpose?* I feared I might scream at him if he didn't speed up. In order not to become even more anxious, I began to make plans for our new lodge.

"Ya do realize, Thom, that we must have a gym and sauna as well as a billiard room?"

"Aye, we can do her." He smiled at me from the front seat.

"We have to furnish plenty of high-quality mountain bikes. Ya do know that's a must?"

"Aye, of course."

"And it would be great to offer clay pigeon shoots. And our guests must be able to fish in the pristine lakes. How many are there, Mr. Wilson?"

Mr. Wilson looked at Thomas with shock. "Well, I don't know right off, but we'll find out soon enough."

"If there aren't already walking trails, we must grade some nice ones. I might plant flowers all over the place to soothe and surprise our guests."

The men glanced at each other again.

"So, we must have several 4x4 vehicles and hire drivers for those who are nor able to walk and bike around the acreage. I mean, it's so extensive that everyone will need some help. Don't ya agree, Mr. Wilson?"

"Yes, indeed, ma'am, whatever ya say."

"I can see our dining room already. I'd like it painted in warm, cheerful colors for our guests. Maybe, a pretty cranberry color would look nice? How many fireplaces, Mr. Wilson? The wedding-cake house and the gold house in Charleston both have six of them. Does Alladale have that many?

"Are there any bears yet? Ya see, at our beach house on Cape San Blas, Florida, we had black bears. They enjoyed raiding our garbage cans at night. Thom, we must restock bears along with wolves. Oh, don't forget coyotes. This entire episode of our lives will be so much fun! I can't wait."

Mr. Wilson appeared to choke then began to cough. I thought he would never stop. Finally, I handed him a cough drop, which helped.

"Ah, when I get a little nervous, I experience this particular cough." Feebly, he looked at my husband while avoiding eye contact with me.

"Of course, we should provide massage therapists. A lovely spa would be welcome, I'm sure. Should we install a golf course? Have I already mentioned these things?"

Thom began to cough. I had never heard him do this, so I passed him a cough drop as well.

"I hope there are plenty of flower gardens in the summer. Maybe, we should add a greenhouse to raise plants. Can ya imagine all the rooms filled with bright, bold flowers, Thom? When your mother visits, she'll love it! And she can give me all sorts of advice. I can't wait to see her!"

"Mr. Wilson, how much farther?" Thom turned pale as he questioned our unhurried driver.

"Hold steady, old man, not much."

"I should start researching which products to offer."

Thom sounded a little scared when he asked, "Products?"

"Yes, silly, for our spa, we must provide only quality items. Of course, we must ask for staff recommendations. Ya probably never considered all of this, did ye, Thom?"

He shook his head and sighed.

"I can just see the entrance. We'll have a large column of natural stones that match the house, with our name tastefully carved. Won't that be lovely?" Both men nodded.

"Did I mention that we must provide a sauna? A nice, comfy one, we want our guests to have every convenience. Right? I found this sweet color, soft apricot, that we should use somewhere in our new home. I still like wallpaper too. Let's have some rooms with stunning wallpapers, right? Paintings and photographs, we'll need lots and lots of those."

"Ah, Mrs. Reid, don't forget, the house comes furnished."

"Yes, of course, I know this silly, but we must make it *ours*, don't ya know? Spectacular light fixtures, we may have to order some of them from Charleston. Do ya recall that place where we purchased so many for the historic home? They had quality, exceptional pieces. Yes, I plan have to contact them right away and ask them to send brochures. I'm ready to get this project started!

"If there's not already a gate, I'd love to have one made with black wrought iron. The drive should be gravel. Don't ya both agree? Oh, I hope all the fireplaces work, like in Charleston. We had six in each of our houses. Did I already mention that? I have so much to do.

"Ya know, let's plan to scatter fire pits all around the property for the cooler weather. We can provide hot spiced cider. There's nothing like a nice fire to warm the spirit. With a piping heated drink, right?

"I'd love to display family pictures. That would mean a great deal to our guests. I'll display photos of Momma and Daddy and yer folks as well. Oh, and we must have some of Max, Elizabeth, and all of their clan. Our coat of arms must proudly hang in a place of honor. Both mine and yours. Right, Thom?

"It sure would be nice to allow people to bring their dogs. I mean, it's not a home without one, right? I feel exhausted. I might stretch out for a moment."

It felt like just seconds later that I heard Thom's voice. "Caroline, wake up! We're approaching Alladale. I don't want ya to miss anything."

We unexpectedly went around a curve in the drive. I felt confused until I saw it. Immediately, I was wide-awake. There stood Alladale in all her glory. The sight took my breath away. I heard the blood in my veins, and it rushed to my ears and my face. I felt hot and flushed, and I struggled to breathe.

The most beautiful Victorian-style home smiled at me on this perfect summer day. The scenery around the estate couldn't have been more dramatic. I almost knocked over poor Mr. Wilson as I rushed toward the massive front door. I reached for the handle.

"Mrs. Reid, the door won't be unlocked. Please wait for me."

I paid no attention but stood awestruck at the entrance because someone had left the door unlocked. At that moment, I spun around as I did when I was a child. *Yes, I have my wedding-cake house back, but it is now a vast castle!*

Chapter Nineteen

It took longer for the wet sheets to dry because the room was so cold. There had been no visits by sparrows or little owls. No one seemed to be aware of me. *Perhaps, my killer has been killed?* My laugh sounded maniacal and shrill.

It's just about over. Aye, I can feel it. It won't end well for ye, Caroline.

What did end well was when Thomas and I met with Molly, Malcolm, and Duncan, ten weeks later, after we purchased Alladale, to celebrate our beautiful new home.

Everyone was amazed that such a complex sale closed in only ten weeks. Usually, it took much longer for an estate as extensive and detailed as this one. The previous owners were aged and wanted to move back to London. We felt sorry for them. After the closing, we went directly to our new home. Feelings of ecstasy overcame us. We took a bottle of champagne for a toast as we stood within our unique estate.

I noticed a new Land Rover sitting in the drive. "Thomas, I think someone is sitting in our drive. Isn't that odd?"

He appeared concerned and strode through the opened door, hastily approaching the car. The previous owners had stopped one more time to say goodbye to the place they had loved for all of their lives. Thom brought them inside.

We felt it was an honor to spend time with these special people. In turn, they kindly provided a wealth of information about the property and exclusive tips on its care. We included them in our toast. They walked parts of the main house with us and explained little idiosyncrasies that we would never have figured out.

After they left, Thom gently held me. "When it's our time to depart this world, I only hope that we can leave it knowing that we did something. Even if it's one thing, and we only helped one soul. Caroline, we must do something worthwhile. Then, we move on to the next adventure. If I've lived a long life, please, don't cry but celebrate my life. Promise me that ye will."

I thought his request was a little morbid but figured that lately, he simply felt overwhelmed with so many emotions surrounding us. The rest of the day, we mostly sat in the drawing-room and looked at the lake. We saw two different species of deer and a red fox. All sorts of birds flew over the water.

"It seems important that we buy several books on birds, for our guests and us. I don't know enough to identify all of these." I motioned with my left hand toward the gathering of birds. Thom agreed.

We admitted that we couldn't wait to move into our rooms in the main lodge and begin construction on the new cottages. When the day turned to twilight, reluctantly, we drove back to our hotel. We planned to move into the Alladale house over the weekend. I wanted to stay there that night, but Thomas wanted to check us out of the hotel first.

The mood inside Bunchrew House Hotel was gay as we walked into its festive spirit. We immediately went to the dining room. In the back, at our favorite table, sat Malcolm, Molly, and Duncan.

"Duncan, you aren't working tonight?"

He smiled. "Aye, I am, but I've taken time off to celebrate with me best friends."

Another waiter, whom I had never seen before, waited on our table while more toasts and celebrations to our spectacular new home were raised. This hotel had been our refuge for over five months. It was a comfortable, easy place to live. I felt a little sad to leave until I thought of Alladale waiting alone.

She pulled at my heart to hurry back. I had already forged a bond with this new place. When I thought of the wedding-cake house, I no longer felt sorrow but joy at this new project and different life. Thomas and I couldn't wait to host our families soon at a gala celebration.

All evening, Duncan acted strangely, appearing nervous. Something was wrong. After Malcolm and Molly left, he remained. *Without a doubt, he wants to speak with us.*

"Okay, Duncan, what's bothering you?" I didn't want anything to dull my joy on this night of new beginnings.

"Look, you're going to hear this when the townspeople realize you're the new owners of Alladale. My uncle, who's a jerk, has wanted to purchase Alladale for some time. The poor guy fell in love with the property over eight months ago but failed organize the proper funds. He sold various properties he owned, as well as stocks, but he just was unable to gather enough cash.

"Last week, he phoned to tell me that he was close to wrapping up the purchase. When I explained that someone from the US had beat him to it, he went ballistic. He's an influential man, accustomed to getting his way. You need to know that he's coming here with the hope of causing problems for you. When I explained your desire to begin a nature reserve, he swore that was his goal and that you had stolen his idea. It's crazy, I know." Sadly, he lowered his head.

As if a light flashed in my head, I recalled a recent time at the paint shop, before the closing, when the owner of the store questioned me about our plans for the lodge. Since we planned to live there, I explained it would be our home first than a business. Also, I shared our ideas of establishing a nature reserve. The proprietor wasn't friendly. When I had seen him around the village a few other times, he stopped in the street and stared at me. It had seemed strange. Something was going on; I could feel it.

"Does your uncle have many friends here? Does he visit often?"

Duncan explained that his uncle owned a small cottage in Inverness and that he had many friends everywhere. "Mr. Malcolm is one of his best."

Thomas and I looked at each other in confusion. "Why didn't Malcolm tell us? He's also one of our best friends. It would have been nice to know this." I tried to conjure up all sorts of reasons for Malcolm's silence on this issue. They all felt contrived.

Duncan had been placed in an awkward position and reverted to his usual behavior. He quickly excused himself and hurried to the front desk.

"Do you remember the man we met when we first came here? He was older, silver-haired, and carried a golden-headed cane. Remember, he mentioned something about being lame?"

"Aye, I remember."

"Don't ask me why, I think this, but I believe he's Duncan's uncle. I have this sixth sense that it's him."

We hurried to the front desk, where Duncan confirmed my suspicions.

"Yes, my uncle was here at that time, but I don't recall a meeting between the two of ya. Umm, this is spooky." Duncan seemed a little fearful of me.

When we returned to our room, Thomas questioned how I could have known. Hesitantly, I confided my strong feelings about certain things. The evening Paula Peterson was killed, I had a feeling that something terrible was going to happen. There were several other times during my life that this intense sensation troubled me. When Paula moved into our neighborhood, I knew she would steal my boyfriend from me. It was such a strong feeling. Also, I felt from a young age that Thomas Baxter Reid and I would marry. Yes, he may have faltered a little during the Paula days, but I always knew we would. On many occasions, as I looked back, a quiet voice had guided me.

What I now felt was a strong certainty that we had an enemy. Someone was out to get us. I knew it. It would not be good what waited for Alladale, Thomas, and me.

From my shackled bed, I called, "Aye, this isn't well."

Chapter Twenty

I refused to deal with drama in the here and now. My fight must be ending. Surely, I deserved to find peace as my struggle began to wane within this lovely chamber of horrors? Once more, I floated back to the past and my final days at Alladale.

The next five years were the happiest time of my life. Our bond with Molly, Malcolm, and Duncan grew stronger. Much of our time gently ticked past, spent with these three who became our family. I felt that I knew almost everything about them. We often played the "Ask Me Three Questions" game—anything you want, I'll answer honestly, but then I get to ask the same of you.

Before long, private things that would never be shared were relinquished with faith in each other. Most of the time, we laughed, but sometimes we cried. Molly replaced Elizabeth in my heart as a sister and best friend. Malcolm and Duncan combined assumed the previous role of Max. I found it endearing that the three of them possessed the same red hair and fair skin. Thomas and I longed to introduce them to our real family finally.

At last, the day we dreamed about arrived. My mind always rushed to this time when I thought of my experiences at Alladale. Max, Elizabeth, and our remaining parents visited us at our new home, arriving the day before our big open-house party. Momma had died years ago, and Josey was unwell and couldn't travel. It was hard to think of the loss of Momma. I often pictured her face and wept. Also, I frequently cried at missing dear Josey, who was like a second mother. Still, on that day, we both filled with anticipation.

They arrived late in the evening before our big event. Thomas and I were exhausted, and the others were so tired from traveling that we barely spoke. On the evening of our open-house party, we met in the drawing-room an hour early with just our family members. Max hadn't changed much at all. Elizabeth had gained a little weight but carried it well. Her lovely raven locks now were threaded with silver, thanks to three young children. Daddy had aged the most after the loss of Momma. He never was the same. The smile I loved still greeted me but not with the former luster. His dark eyes appeared sad, almost confused. Mr. and Mrs. Reid remained hilarious and pleased me with only small changes. I smiled each time I recalled looking through her gown so long ago. As we huddled closely together, it was as though we had never been apart.

Thomas and I had joined the local Methodist church, along with Molly and Malcolm. Duncan attended the Catholic one. We had invited many of the congregation. Our small Scottish church family provided peace and guidance for us. We still enjoyed a little whisky but not to the level of that night long ago when I promised myself never to become intoxicated again. The earlier feeling of doom that something terrible was about to happen remained tucked in the folds of my mind, but I seldom felt the nagging sensation.

"Well, anyway, I saw ol' Uncle Robert on the street in downtown Charleston about two months ago. The ugly cuss hadn't changed a bit!"

We all howled with laughter because Uncle Robert was a most handsome man. The news that he and Jack Abernathy were gay had become official, although the subject had been discussed for some time.

"I'm glad that the beautiful Kayce decided not to marry him. Thank God Mark came along at the right time. Her life might not have been so happy, and there wouldn't be a Caroline!"

Daddy smiled, "I always had my suspicions. I'm glad they made it official. Didn't the two marry or something?"

Max confirmed they had.

An hour later, the guests began to arrive. Everyone glowed on this memory-making evening. A professional photographer snapped impromptu pictures among the unsuspecting crowd. We also captured a few group shots. My husband had never looked as happy as when we took everyone on a tour of our beautiful home. We presented the main house to them, but they were also free to venture around the grounds. We had over a dozen golf carts to carry those who wanted to travel a little deeper into the forest.

Molly and Elizabeth appeared amazed at how their earlier lives were similar. Duncan followed Max around as if he were a rock star. Malcolm and my daddy stood together, talking for hours, sharing a bottle of whisky, and laughing. I wondered what secrets passed between them.

It was late fall, so there was a bit of chilliness in the air. All six fireplaces were lit and filled the house with warmth and the smell of oak, but it was hard to heat such an old building.

It was a magical night that would live in our memories forever. The trickling laughter from our friends and families made me feel a little sad. I wished that Josey had come; I missed her. Her face filled my thoughts.

Just then, Max ambled toward me with a smile. "Caroline, Josey asked me to deliver a message to you. She wants you to know that she loves you as much as her own children and that upon leaving this old world, which doesn't appear far away—this is difficult to put into words—she told me to tell you that 'ol' Sissy Smothers won't be enjoying her passing.' I couldn't make much sense of it, but she said you would know."

I threw back my head and laughed with abandon. "Yes, I know what she means."

Daddy strolled over to us, finally able to move away from Malcolm's allure. "Did Max tell you what Josey said?"

I smiled.

"Well, she told me to tell you to remember her as she was and not venture away from this place. Josey says, 'Life is too short to mourn the dead. We should love those who are living.' I think she doesn't want you to come back to Charleston because she's sick. I'm not sure, but that's what I believe."

"She's saying exactly that, and I must honor her wishes. Remember how upset she gets when someone doesn't?"

"Aye, I do! She's gotten worse over the year without ya."

Was there something in the blood of the Scottish people that they resorted to the language of their past when they came together? Thomas and Malcolm wore their kilts. At the end of the evening, Max had changed into one of Thomas's and tried to dance a jig but not very well. Still, he did a better job than his brother. Malcolm called us around him, explaining that he had carried out a little research on Alladale because he also had fallen in love with her grandeur. "Let me tell you," he smiled, "this is the home of the eccentric."

According to our friend, the Romans once referred to this region as "the Great Forest of Caledon." He pointed out that because of the hillside's bleakness, that was no longer the case.

"If ya want to know eccentric, let me introduce you to Lady Meux. That one makes all of us look perfectly sane.

"Valerie, this former actress, and banjo-playing barmaid married up for herself when she became the wife of Sir Henry Meux, third baronet (1856-1900). While performing in Brighton, she was given an additional title.

"Mrs. Meux stated, 'I can honestly say that my sins were committed before, not after marriage.'

"You can call her what you want, but I bloody well say she had a great deal of gumption. Who else would drive their four-wheeled carriage pulled by two zebras?

"The great wealth of the Meux family came from their brewery empire. After being snubbed by the entire lot of Sir Henry's crowd, this daughter of a Devon butcher constantly drove past the Marquess of Ailesbury's home, the wife of Henry's father, the 2nd baronet.

"Valerie also sat for James McNeil Whistler—an American and one of the most acclaimed and expensive society painters of the day. What she couldn't charm her way into, she was able to purchase.

"Sir Henry and Lady Meux took a lease of Alladale when they fell in love with the Highlands and the bewitching scenery. At that time, Alladale was one of the best-known deer forests in Scotland. Sir Charles Ross, the famous Ross rifle's inventor, was the owner and lived at nearby Balnagown Castle. A very renowned person now owns that property. I refuse to name drop.

"Just as you have dreamed of someday owning a place where you might provide stalking, fishing, and grouse shooting for your friends and patrons, Henry and Valerie did as well.

"The fabulously wealthy Maharaja Holkar of Indore brought such a large entourage with him that an extension had to be added to the rear of the lodge to accommodate them. He was also next in line for Alladale. So, you see, my dearest friends, your dreams for this magical place have been felt by many others. Caroline, when you speak of eccentricity, you have called this one correctly. However, don't forget that many here think of you as being what you label others. There is a long and tattered history to those who loved this place and this country."

At one point, Molly braided Elizabeth's dark hair into a Celtic braid. She looked gorgeous. We recorded most of the evening with a digital camera and promised to send copies to everyone.

Alladale glowed on this night of her christening. Daddy kept saying he couldn't believe that Thom and I lived in a "sandcastle in the snow." The three of us discussed the miserable day when my future husband attempted his first construction in the sand.

Five days later, our family members flew back to the US. I thought I'd feel sadness, but I didn't. Instead, great peace surrounded us and our home as we prepared to open the lodge for guests next year. With only a few weeks before the weather turned frigid, we decided to wait until winter passed since the heavy snow could hamper our guests' arrival. We planned to open early the following spring. Thom and I looked forward to our first winter by the fire, and long walks into the forest. The isolation failed to frighten me. There was plenty to keep me busy. Already, I searched recipes for hearty stews and soups.

We had as yet been unable to fulfill all of our dreams. Thom's goal, to create a fenced/controlled wolf reserve, had not come to fruition, but he promised never to cease dreaming of their return, as well as bringing back bear, elk, and lynx, although they were not a targeted species.

"If Yellowstone National Park can do this, surely, we Scots can as well."

A few nights after our gala, we stood by a large window staring at the moon over our sparkling lake. "Caroline, can you hear it?"

I listened but heard nothing. "No, what?"

"Sometimes, I declare, I can hear the call of the wild. I hear the beautiful sound of those who were forced from this land. I can hear the cry of the wolf. Am I going mad?"

"No, my love, you may be the only sane one left. Look at the mess we've made of our planet. There's still time to make a difference. Yet here in Scotland, some fear losing their right to walk freely more than destruction to our environment. You're right. If Yellowstone can do it, Scotland can bloody-well make it happen. If only they understood your dreams."

Chapter Twenty-One

Two weeks after our fete, on September 15, Max called early one morning, "Hey, Caroline, are you up?"

I wasn't. "Max, you must have forgotten the time difference. But I'm up now—no big deal. Thom's already outside doing something, what's going on there?"

"Caroline, I've got bad news for you. You need to sit down."

I explained that I had been expecting this call about Josey and had prepared for it.

"Caroline, it's not about Josey. It's—" He began to cry. "Caroline, your father is gone."

I almost asked, "Gone where?" as I had when Josey called me years earlier to report Momma's death. I sat down. Outside, Thom waved as he walked past the window.

He appeared normal. *Doesn't the world know that a great man has left this earth? How can life continue as before?* No tears fell. The feeling was numbness and denial that this was happening. It just couldn't; *Daddy can't be gone.*

"You should know that I was with him. He died peacefully, but he said the same thing as Josey about ol' Sissy Smothers. Who is this woman? Is she the Grim Reaper or something? Y'all are a little frightening."

"Max, Thom and I won't be coming to Charleston. Our attorney received all the details pertaining to Daddy's death much earlier before Momma passed. Daddy wants to be buried beside Momma. That's all there is to it. How's Josey?"

"Not good, our friend is barely hanging on. I don't know whether to tell her about your dad."

"Don't tell her. It won't do any good. I love you and hate to leave you dealing with this, but we're an odd family, I guess."

Max explained that he completely understood my desires and feelings. He said that he wished he could deal with death like my family. "You know we all fly to see someone we love when they die. Everyone says they need closure, but what provides more closure than death?"

Dear Max said that sometimes he regretted never leaving Charleston and all the drama. We ended on a happy note, and I fell into my soft lavender wingback chair. Thomas waved again from outside the window. He was cutting wood for the winter. I couldn't wait to open the lodge next year after our winter closure of January and February.

"Come on, March. I'll be so ready for your arrival, and finally opening our lodge for guests." For a moment, I smiled as I tried to absorb the latest news about my father.

I always began my day with prayer and reading scripture. My special prayers for Daddy and Josey that day brought me peace. But as I stood with thoughts of them firmly in mind, the phone rang again.

Once more, Max's tearful voice came through the line. "Oh, dearest Caroline, you are so brave. I hate to tell you this." I waited.

"Caroline, Josey just died. After our call, I went next door. She asked me if Mr. Mark was gone. I couldn't lie to her. When I told her that he had only just died an hour earlier, she smiled. 'Well, it's time for me to leave now.' She closed her big, brown eyes and was gone. She died so peacefully. They both did."

Once more, I wasn't able to cry or even feel anything. Instead, I listened to Max grieve. Morosely, I sat in my comfy lavender chair and watched Thom acting goofy outside. Hours passed. I made no effort to move. Instead, I remembered all the people who had filled my life up to this point. Every member of my immediate family had now departed, except Uncle Robert. He wasn't really family. The more I thought of him, the more I detested him. I hated to say it, but I considered it a shame that Daddy died, but my mother's useless brother still walked the earth, creating havoc somewhere.

Finally, I went to kneel by the window, and my tears fell freely. Lovingly I recalled my magical childhood with the three best parents; I considered Josey as a second mother. Additional time slowly passed as their memories made me laugh and cry.

At last, Thomas came inside. "Sorry to bother ya, Caroline. Are ya still talking to God?" He smiled.

"No, we're finished. HE told me to remind ya of HIS love for you." I returned his grin with a watery one of my own.

His arms enfolded me, and he lifted me from my knees. The smell of pine mixed with the freshness of the outdoors filled my lungs as I deeply breathed in his heavenly scent. We stood there, wrapped in our own thoughts until I told him of the two phone calls from Max.

Sadly, he nodded. "Aye, yer daddy told me that he expected to leave this world soon. Caroline, Mark didn't explain that he had liver cancer? Once he told me, I noticed the beginning of jaundice."

"No, he never told me, but it's okay. What could I have done? Josey has also gone to Heaven. She and Daddy are up there having a party with Momma. I wonder if God gave them a shot of whisky?"

Thom smiled. "Well, I'll make our flight reservations and all the plans."

"No need, Daddy doesn't want to provide ol' Sissy Smothers the pleasure of another funeral, ya know? Neither does Josey. Max is handling the details."

"Aye, ol' Sissy Smothers again, is it? Well, he did mention that ye would know what to do. Are ya sure, Caroline?"

"Aye, except I'm goin' to request that some of his ashes be sent to me. I want to spread them over the land here. Right there, by the lake where ye were working. Isn't it funny that all of our lives, we plan for death? I mean, we all know it's coming for us and those we love. Yet, when it happens, we're shocked. I think that losing Paula at such a young age prepared me differently than others for this process. I'm fine. I'll miss all three of them for the rest of me life, but I know they would want me to live a meaningful life. What more is there? Isn't this what God instructs? Will ya walk with me? I need to smell the freshness of outdoors."

"Aye, I'd walk with ye anywhere, even death."

He couldn't have known the truth of his words.

Chapter Twenty-Two

My mind attempted to keep a chronological sequence inside my death chamber, but the last five years now meshed together. It was impossible to keep them in order. During the winter months, we had worked non-stop in preparation for our Grand Opening scheduled on the first day of spring, March 25. That time was very clear to me. There had been much to do. Earlier, we had hired Natasha Buttigieg as our chef. Her impeccable reputation impressed us. She practiced on us each day so that she could create a menu and present dishes that we approved for our guests. This extraordinary lady fed us well during the winter months. Also, we hired our general manager, Pieter-Paul Groenhuiggsen, who lived on the property. It was wonderful having him close, especially during those two desolate months.

Our location at Alladale was on the narrowest point of Britain and the most remote. Having a few of our staff during this isolated period helped us feel secure. It was easy to relinquish control to members of the team who were confident and well-trained.

Because of our location, on a clear day, residents and guests of Alladale could observe both the east and west coasts of our beloved Scottish home. Often, as we stood beholding those treacherous waters, I thought about the works of one of Scotland's most celebrated writers. This literary genius from Edinburgh was born on November 13, 1850, and had delighted my childhood days with his unforgettable tales: The Master of Ballantrae, Kidnapped, Treasure Island, The Strange Case of Dr. Jekyll and Mr. Hyde, as well as A Child's Garden of Verses, Robert Louis Stevenson was a prodigy of unparalleled skill.

Often on blustery evenings, I now awoke in the middle of the night with a shiver. I had done the same when I was a child. Thoughts of Treasure Island continued to evoke a melancholy feeling in me.

Charleston, too, had ties with pirates. When I was a little girl, I frequently dreamed of becoming a pirate and sailing with the likes of William Kidd, Blackbeard, and Edward England. Now, whenever I thought of those scoundrels, I thought of Uncle Robert, who was a misfit in his family. Tears gently fell when I recalled my beloved Momma, Daddy, and Josey buried in the family plot. *Ol' Robert won't be welcomed there.*

Max was able to get some of Daddy's and Josey's ashes, which we scattered around Alladale. I wished that I had thought to get some of Momma's as well. During this secluded time, we prepped the existing trails inside the nature reserve and made new ones. Thom began work with an excellent builder on two new cottages, the Eagles Craig and Ghillie's Rest. It would take ten years to complete everything, but all of this planning and activity excited us. When we climbed into bed at night, we fell asleep quickly. I entertained dreams of pirates, and my beloved husband's thoughts were, no doubt, inside this place, which stirred our emotions and provided tremendous tranquility.

171

Our location, being about an hour and a half from Inverness, allowed easy access to stores. Through supporting the local businesses, we gained acceptance into the tight community. Promptly, invitations to parties and other social events arrived. It was as though we had always lived in Inverness. Molly and Malcolm joined us several times each week to enjoy a feast prepared by Natasha. The four of us, with Duncan, had our little circle of friends.

Often, I frequented Molly's Mole, the eclectic shop of my dear friend. The store suited me. Each time I visited, she surprised me with intriguing objects from all over the world. I already had made purchases for the two cottages, which hadn't yet begun construction. My Audi Q5 arrived back at Alladale stuffed with treasures for the lodge and upcoming cabins.

Thomas and Pieter-Paul groaned when I arrived. Once our entire project was finished, Alladale would consist of two lodges and two cottages nestled among 23,000 acres. We offered glens, brightly colored hillsides, shining waters packed with salmon, trout, and Atlantic sturgeon. Plus, all meals were provided. Thinking about all we offered, plus the hills, lochs, and native wildlife, I considered booking a room for myself. I chuckled at my wit.

With the loss of Momma, Josey, and Elizabeth, although she was still alive, from my life, not to mention my childhood friend, Paula, I was starved for the company of a female friend. Duncan, Malcolm, and Pieter-Paul kept me laughing, but there was something about another woman's friendship that nothing else could fill. Molly had closed that void.

After our Open House, Molly's talent at Celtic braiding spread around the area of Inverness. Women rushed to Molly's Mole, requesting her skill in creating a relaxed look. She had added that to her repertoire. Molly told me she would always be grateful to me for introducing her to Elizabeth. She and Malcolm planned a visit to Charleston next year.

Molly's delightful, unique store filled with the scent of spice from burning candles. This little place was a shop that women adored. One cold day, as I sat by the fire inside, Molly received a call from Malcolm saying that he needed her right away.

Instead of her closing the space, I volunteered to handle the register. *What fun it will be away from the planning and questions of the bustling Alladale.* Thomas must have stayed awake every night to compile a long list of things for me because each day, that's what waited. With peaceful music playing and a gentle fire burning, in her cute shop, it felt like a vacation to me. I took the opportunity to go through my friend's merchandise.

A local acquaintance, Gwynevere Peterson, rushed into the shop. "Aye, Caroline, have ya seen the papers? Yer in them, ya know."

Gwynevere was a large, silver-haired woman who lived in town. I didn't know her well, but she was nice to Thom and me. There was always a protective spirit about her. She produced a copy of the Inverness Courier and poked it in my face.

I groaned at the interruption. "What is it, Gwynevere? What in this world can be so earth-shattering?"

"Well, ya need to read it. Ye'll be angry enough. That crazy little boy-man is doing this to ya." She sighed as she shook the paper in my face.

Reluctantly, I took the paper. I had hoped for peace on this lonely dark day. And there it was! Big as life, Duncan proclaimed his love to none other than me for the entire community to see! He had written a letter explaining his respect and admiration. Then, he published it online. Someone who saw it, copied it, and sent it to the paper. Undoubtedly, there would be more to the story. Already, I dreaded walking down the street and hearing the giggles and feeling the stares. *Will they think I encouraged him?* I was furious. While I decided to close the shop and rush home, the phone rang.

"So, my wife's in love with the young Duncan, is she?" Thomas howled with laughter.

"Ya think this is funny? I'm livid. I'll kill him when I see him."

"Aye, that would be tonight 'cause he's coming here to Alladale for supper with Malcolm and Molly. He wants to speak with ya. Hold on."

"Ms. Caroline, I'm so sorry. I chan eil fios agam."

"Duncan, don't speak in Gaelic!"

"Okay. Honestly, I may have gone a little overboard, but it didn't sound quite so mushy when I wrote it on the internet. I thought ye'd be pleased with the publicity. I was hoping it might drive some business to ya. I know yer angry, but I'm humiliated. Everyone's snickering behind me back. It's bloody well awful, ya know?" He sighed.

Laughing with great glee, I fell back into the comfy yellow chair that Molly kept by the window. Mrs. Peterson grabbed her newspaper and scurried away.

"Now, my love, don't ye be angry with this lad." Thomas had captured the phone again. "He meant ya no harm. Remember the wise words of someone. I believe them to be from King James I of England, when he said, 'No news is better than evil news.' Now, I ask ya, is this evil? Ye should thank young Duncan because he's set everybody's tongues awaggin'. All of this is good for us."

"Aye, indeed! Tell Duncan that later we'll give them something about which to chatter. All is well."

Soon enough, we did give the town something to talk about; it wasn't good news.

Chapter Twenty-Three

I was well-aware that the end of my story was near. As hard as I tried to rush my thoughts ahead or jump to the last days before I ended up here, my mind wouldn't cooperate. It seemed intent on making me relive most of my life. I no longer bothered to open my eyes. That act created pain. The heavy crust over my eyes tore the delicate eye tissue.

Easily, my story continued in my tired mind. Each winter day, especially on the coldest ones, I dedicated my time to searching for needed items to stock the lodge. After growing tired of this, I started researching Scotland. I wanted to know everything about this place that I loved.

I discovered that Scotland covered the northern third of the isle of Great Britain. Most of our part of the island remained surrounded by the Atlantic Ocean, save the ninety-six miles bordering the UK. The North Sea touched our northeast side while the Irish Sea graced our southern one. Seven hundred and ninety islands were a part of our land. In 320 BC, a Greek sailor, Pytheas, first mentioned the island. He referred to the northern tip of Britain as "Orcas." Many Gaelic-speaking clerics, working as missionaries, are believed to have begun the Gaelic influence. Things really became interesting for me when I learned that during the eighth century, Vikings started to raid Scotland in search of slaves, but they mainly wanted the land.

After I read that, I ran to the window to check for distinctive Viking ships. Any reference to pirates and Vikings caught my attention. When I thought of Uncle Robert, I felt certain that Vikings' blood must course through my veins. Uncle Robert was the greediest person I'd ever known. He only seemed concerned with taking away from others. Two attacks on my family, and I wondered with Momma and Daddy gone, would he again attempt to hijack me?

I was never able to completely grasp the history of the country that I now called my own because Scotland's history was long and complicated. During the Middle Ages, Scotland was an independent kingdom that won several wars against England. In 1603, James VI, a Scot, became king of England and Ireland, which established a union of the three kingdoms of Scotland, Ireland, and England. The Scottish people were given a chance to vote for independence a few years ago but chose to remain part of the UK.

The bagpipe hails from ancient Egypt, according to some historians. Others credit it as being Irish. The origin of the kilt remains controversial. Some say it originated in Scotland. Others say it's from Ireland. The prevailing thought seems to be that Thomas Rowlinson, a Quaker from Lancashire, takes the credit. As in all things Scottish, there is significant controversy. Edinburgh is the capital, while the largest city is Glasgow.

My mind longed to understand this diverse and complex country. Many facts, even simple ones, were easily debatable.

Tonight, inside my icy tomb, I considered that my heart remained here, with this place I loved.

Chapter Twenty-Four

At last, our targeted date of March 25 arrived. Not only was it the first day of spring, but it was also our "big" day. Since the moment we purchased Alladale, we had marketed it for the tourist season. I was so excited and bolted from the bed. Thomas had worked especially hard the previous day, so I let him sleep.

I dressed quickly and rushed to the computer to check and verify our bookings. It promised to be a grand opening season with the maximum capacity of fifteen guests scheduled for our first week. That was wonderful. Thom had a knack for clever marketing, and we had hired the best in the business to get the word out over the internet. Eventually, after we added two cottages, we hoped to accommodate thirty guests.

Natasha greeted me with a smile and a large cup of coffee. "You have to begin with a proper breakfast before you rush off."

The smell of eggs mixed with freshly roasted coffee beans drew me to my place at the table. I was taking my first bite when Thomas sauntered into the room.

"Do ya have another of those breakfasts hidden somewhere?" In minutes, Natasha set a beautiful plate in front of him.

He sat beside me and leaned over to kiss me. "Are ye ready, Caroline, the belle of Charleston, soon to become the belle of Scotland?"

Castles in the Snow

My heart still fluttered after six years of marriage. All things in our future appeared bright. The day passed quickly as a truck full of fresh flowers arrived to fill the public and private rooms. We distributed them to the various chambers. Immediately, the delightful fragrance of heather drifted through the house. We tried to use only native plants but couldn't help mixing a few roses and lilies, as well as some rare orchids, among the arrangements.

Malcolm and Molly visited before lunch with a present for our gala opening. Molly had selected a few of my favorite pieces from her store. Before they left, Duncan appeared with boxes of fresh fruit for our guests. Many other locals stopped in with treasures they valued to share with our visitors. Thankfully, Mrs. Robertson supplied a giant welcome mat for the front door. I thought I had purchased everything but had forgotten this critical item. We were very "hands-on" in the early days and covered every detail concerning the running of Alladale ourselves.

A little early, our first visitors checked in at 2:30, an older couple. They touched everything as they praised our hard work. From the looks of things, we were more than prepared. Mouthwatering aromas from the kitchen greeted me each time I entered the shining, happy lobby. It was beyond my wildest dreams. I had set up a display of my books for our guests' enjoyment. Already, several had been snatched from the table. Thom and I felt like celebrities because everyone wanted to meet us and question us about our success. A few even asked for our autographs.

The local paper arrived with cameras flashing behind it, as did a famous magazine from another country. Max and Elizabeth phoned to wish us "Deagh Fhortan," Gaelic for "Good Fortune." A spectacular arrangement of giant flowers arrived while we spoke with them. When I read the card, I cried because they had been able to arrange their call as the most beautiful flowers imaginable were delivered to us. Max and his wife had always created happiness for me. Such kindness made it feel as if they were here with us.

Alladale's polished looks became her, as did so many admiring strangers roaming her halls. Outside, people were already walking in the late afternoon sunshine. The weather could not have been more perfect. We reached a balmy 50 degrees Fahrenheit. From all the happy guests, you would have thought we were having a heatwave.

"Aye, Alladale is bringing good fortune to us all," someone crooned in the lobby.

Outside, our reservations manager, Innes MacNeil, a local, smiled from ear to ear as he busily answered questions and provided information. People appeared starved to learn all about us and this property, which stole many hearts. All the months of planning had been well-spent.

In the house, Remi Bacznski rushed around as though he had been working here for years. It was difficult to believe this was only our first day. Thom and I expected all sorts of goofs and problems, but they didn't happen. We felt proud of our multi-cultural staff. Each member was chosen with a great deal of thought.

Chef Natasha personally delivered our dinner on the first evening. Thom and I sat at a small table in the back of the dining room where we gloated. Every dish was local and organic. From fresh and wild-caught seafood or trout to culled wild venison, whatever each person had ordered, they quieted when they began to savor the tastes. Our state-of-the-art aquaponic gardens and exterior raised beds of vegetables, salad greens, herbs, and berries demonstrated the degree of perfection we sought to deliver. Nothing was too good for those who chose Alladale.

At the end of a most auspicious day, we stood in our suite, staring out at the lake. The open window allowed wafts of fresh air to filter inside gently. The distant sounds of a calling bird made me think of the hauntingly lovely golden eagle. Thanks to the conservation charity RSPB Scotland, it had been chosen as our national bird. Any time a species was saved from extinction, Thom and I thanked God for the many who cared enough to champion it. Far in the distance, the hoot of an owl declared its presence.

"I wish Momma and Daddy, as well as Josey, could have seen us tonight. They would have been proud."

"Aye, I didn't want to dampen the high spirits, but my mum called earlier. It seems Dad is very ill. She is tough as nails, ya know? She said to tell ye that ol' Sissy Smothers won't be takin' in the sight of her and me dad. I don't want ye to worry. All's well, dear Caroline."

When he fell asleep, I kneeled beside the bed and prayed for all those I loved who had departed, and for Thom's family. Mr. and Mrs. Reid were my mentors. They loved me just like my parents. It would be hard to face the future without them standing quietly in the shadows.

Chapter Twenty-Five

Max phoned to tell us that Elizabeth had just delivered their new baby, number four. "You should see her, Caroline. She looks for all the world like you. When she smiles, her little face wrinkles up like yours, we named her Caroline Emma Reid, just like you. I'll bet that someday, she will be called 'the belle of Charleston!'

"Elizabeth is crying. She always becomes very emotional after giving birth, but she keeps saying that she misses you. I shouldn't have told you. There's nothing to be done about it. We want you to know that we both miss you and Thom." He quickly wrapped up the call. I felt a pang of homesickness.

Awareness that I had almost reached the end of my memories produced little fear. In the beginning, I feared that once I arrived at this point, at the end of my recollections, I would die alone inside my beautiful chamber of horrors.

"I'm ready now. If only I could know what happened to Thom and who did this to us. It's okay, Jesus. I know it will be clear someday. I'm ready to go now—no more fighting."

The first moment of the end of my life now grabbed hold of me. Determination gripped me. If I was able to stay alive, I might figure out who was doing this. Slowly, I replayed the exact moment the craziness had begun.

###

I had noticed that a guest room in one of the cottages needed a little touch-up paint. Hurriedly, I set off on the hour and a half drive to the paint store. It was early summer, on June 15.

"Good morning, how's everything?" I greeted the owner.

He had never been friendly, but I had grown used to his sour disposition.

"I only need one gallon of that cranberry color. What's it called? Ye have all the colors written down for us."

"If ya don't know the color, I can't be lookin' everythin' up for ya all the time. What's the color that ya need, madam?"

His grumpy words floored me. We had purchased all the paint and wallpaper for Alladale, plus many other articles from him. We'd spent a hefty amount. He hadn't minded looking things up for us back when the money flowed so easily. I was speechless while everyone looked at me and lowered their eyes. I knew something was going on, but what?

"Okay, well, let me look at the colors. Maybe, I'll remember the name from your list."

He frowned at me while I looked down the list, but I finally located the correct color. By now, the other customers had left.

"Here it is, right here." I handed him the swatch.

"Ya can pick it up in two days, but ya should call before coming. It might not be ready."

I pushed him about the reason for such a delay. "Ye always mix the paint on the same day. There aren't any other customers. It would help me not to have to drive back in two days."

"That's not my concern, now, is it? There's a line of names before ya. Ye must wait yer turn. Don't ya be struttin' in here acting like ya own the place. Ya don't! Others would have liked to buy the property ye snapped up. It's not right if ya ask me." He turned and walked away, entering a private space in the back.

I slowly walked outside. The day was warm and sunny. The fresh scent of the outdoors usually created a smile, but today, I just felt shocked. Never had I been treated so rudely. *Why?* This incident made no sense to me. I wasn't one to be brushed aside, so I confidently strode back inside.

Mr. Wallace stood with his back to me. He laughed loudly. "Aye, ya should have seen her face. It was priceless. I tell ye, it was priceless. When I finish with her and her fancy husband, they'll not be so cocky."

I stood there, listening to him and wearing a "cocky" smile.

When he turned, he gasped. "What're ya doin' comin' back in here? I've told ya two days. Ye need to learn to listen to us, Missie."

He looked ridiculous, standing before me with his face gathered into a huge reddish pucker. Now, I understand what is happening. I didn't know why, but it was evident that he was trying to intimidate me.

"Mr. Wallace, I know that ye've never liked me, which is fine. Ya see, I don't care. It does amaze me that after the volume of business we've given ya, there isn't some rapport between us. What's changed?"

He looked shocked. "'What's changed?' Ya have the nerve to ask me, 'what's changed?' Let me tell ya. Any woman who would lead on a young man, the way you've done with that lad, Duncan, well, I don't think much of her, especially one that's married."

Once again, he moved away; his head held high. Anger overwhelmed me that he dared to be so smug. I rang the little bell sitting on the counter.

"Ya need to go on now! I'm busy. I've nothing more to say to ya. There's someone important on the way!" He frowned heavily.

"That may be so, but I want ye to know that we have several friends in this town. I'll ask them to purchase my paint, so whenever ye fill an order in the future, ya won't know if it's for that person or if they're buying for us. Furthermore, I want ya to know this: Neither my 'fancy husband' nor I will be botherin' ya in the future." Holding my head high, I turned on my heel and stomped away from him. I returned to lay the color swatch on the counter and smiled sweetly at him. He looked dumbfounded.

Molly's store wasn't busy, so I stopped to visit. After I explained what happened, she looked confused. Neither Thom nor I had ever mentioned Duncan's earlier words when he had mentioned Malcolm being friends with his uncle. Although the news bothered us, we decided to give Malcolm the benefit of the doubt and hoped that he might explain it to us soon. I considered that as I stood before my friend, desiring words of comfort.

"Really? This doesn't make any sense, does it? Mr. Wallace has always been friendly to us. Maybe it's because you're from another country? I don't know. He's never said anythin' to me."

Her sympathetic smile made me feel a little better. Soon, we talked and laughed as we always did. We made some future plans.

I didn't mean to stay long. There was a list of things to do back at Alladale. As I rushed to my car, I spied the silver-haired man we had met on our arrival at the Bunchrew House Hotel. Although years older than I, he was nice-looking and dressed impeccably. In the late afternoon sun, his silver hair glistened with vitality. Today, he wore a tartan kilt with a dark shirt.

When he saw me, he became animated, "Is it ye? The girl from the hotel? Ya live here now, do ye? Ya bought the property of my friend, now, did ye?

If ya see a red-haired girl, well, ye'll know the end is near."

He hurled those words into the street.

It seemed odd that I hadn't seen him again until *this* day when I had a confrontation with the proprietor of the paint store, who had mentioned: "expecting someone important." Once again, the strange man seemed to disappear into the air. A line of cars hurried past, and he was gone.

Now, what's he trying to tell me? Is he a friend or foe?

Thankfully, I turned toward home, sanity, and love.

Chapter Twenty-Six

Get ready, old girl, the end is near at last. There's no prolonging or denying it. You can get angry and bargain with God, but it's ending here, now. I can feel it.

There was little life remaining in my tired, old body. It was just as well. I was ready for the close of my chapter. For a while now, I hoped the final moments were near. *How long might I lie here until someone finds my frozen dead body? Maybe not until the staff returns.* I hated that they would be greeted with my decaying mess. I briefly smiled as I remembered long ago when everyone I loved had referred to me as stinking.

"Well, they should smell you today! The stench is pretty potent."

My mind moved backward to a few days earlier. Late on a Friday, as Thom and I strolled the land, we noticed that someone had stolen our entrance sign. I particularly loved it due to its simplistic design. My husband had wanted a large, fancy sign to greet our visitors. It took a great deal of persuading for me to get this one that appeared austere.

"Thom, did you do something with the entrance sign? It's gone."

He was laughing at my outraged demeanor, but then he turned. He appeared as surprised as I was. "No, I haven't done anything to it. Maybe Pieter-Paul? We'll ask him after our walk."

Both of us felt a little confused. When we had first arrived in Scotland, everyone appeared friendly and accommodating. *What had changed?* We tried to decipher the meaning of it all. I explained about Mr. Wallace's statement, which implied that I had seduced young Duncan. I, a married woman, had supposedly attempted to "start an affair with the boy."

"Aye, although he said that, come on, it makes no sense. He must be smarter than that?"

We laughed, but it didn't feel funny. For a few hours, we walked peacefully in that glorious June evening. The crunch of tires on the gravel caused us both to turn. Pieter-Paul was returning from the village.

"Aye, Caroline, I have yer paint. Mr. Wallace didn't have a clue it was for ye. At least, if he did, he didn't say anythin' to me."

I laughed. *Life is too short to let these senseless incidents upset me. I won't allow it.* Thom asked about the entrance sign.

"Aye, it's been gone for two days. I figured ya had changed it." He nodded at me because he had earlier agreed with Thom that the sign should be more significant. He drove away slowly, so as not to stir the dust.

When we returned home, most of the guests had gone to bed. Natasha served us an elegant dinner. We stopped by the tall window to watch the sunset over our lake. On this particularly lovely night, it seemed a shame to let anything upset us. I smiled as Thom gently hugged me. A loud thud shook us back to reality.

"What was that?" He pulled away from me.

Together, we rushed to the front door and opened it. A rock with a paper wrapped around it lay nearby. The hit resulted in damage to the paint on the door. Thom picked it up and looked carefully around the property. There was no sign of anything or anyone. He carried the large rock inside. The paper was held in place by a piece of twine. When he unwrapped it, he handed the note to me. The words I read caused me to swallow.

"If ya see a red-haired girl, well, ye'll know the end is near."

Is the whole place insane, or is it just us?

Thom questioned me about its meaning; I didn't have a clue. Afterward, we began to ask our friends, but they didn't know. Three days later, we once again walked toward the entrance. The walk down to the main road from our gate was a pleasant one. When we returned, I noticed the missing sign was back in the correct place near the entrance. We scratched our heads and returned home.

Malcolm and Molly, accompanied by Duncan, joined us for dinner. They all appeared surprised when we shared these strange occurrences. No one could be more shocked than I. Evidently; we had an enemy, maybe more than one. The realization that someone had it in for us didn't bide well. We had invested a great deal in our new home and desired peace. I briefly considered returning to Charleston to see the precious Caroline Emma Corbett, who soon would run down the long halls of the spectacular gold house on The Battery.

The thought of Mrs. Reid holding the little girl as she once had me created a deep longing. That memory transported me to the very moment when I understood the power of nurturing. How comforting it felt when she allowed me to climb onto her lap one day when I felt ill. She cradled me with such love. *Oh, how I wish that Daddy, Momma, or Josey was alive to guide me in this crazy situation. What have I done to create enemies?*

The next morning, I was aware of the constant ringing of the phone. "Remi, what's going on? Wow! There have been so many reservations."

"Yes, there have been quite a few, but many of the calls are hang-ups."

I wasn't sure what he meant. He asked if he should have the line checked.

"No, I don't know who it is or why they're doing this, but I believe I understand a little more about what's happening. Someone has it in for us. This person is attempting to intimidate us, but I won't allow it!"

Remi appeared alarmed. "I advise you to use caution, Miss Caroline. I don't like the sound of this."

I described the silver-haired man who always repeated the same sentence. Remi had never seen or heard of such a person and didn't know what his strange words meant.

Thomas and I enjoyed attempting small repairs and renovations inside the lodge, as we had done in our historic home inside The Battery. That afternoon, I worked on simple paint touch-ups. It was a fun process that provided instant gratification. It took me all afternoon to finish my project.

Malcolm and my husband had gone earlier for a quick pint at Johnny Foxes. The fresh summer air pushed through the open window, and I stretched out on the sofa for a nap. When the doorbell rang, I leaped from my place. I wasn't aware that my nerves were frazzled, but apparently, they were. I must have slept about an hour because the aromas of dinner wafted gently through the air.

When I opened the door, a local florist shop's delivery man stared at me, "Mrs. Caroline Emma Corbett Reid?"

The young man before me was tall with blond hair. The intensity of his blue eyes immediately caught my attention. I smiled. He did not. He wore a professional uniform of white slacks and shirt.

"I've got to tell ya that everyone back at the shop is confused by this. Did ye place this order?" He lowered his eyes.

My mind was filled with cobwebs from my nap. I shook my head, attempting to clear them. His words made no sense to me.

"I don't think so. We have many flowers in our garden with the arrival of summer. Just the tremendous amount of heather can fill our lodge."

Again, I attempted a smile, but he didn't return it. I felt a chilliness from the young man. I recognized him. He had delivered flowers to us many times.

"Well, if ya didn't, I believe I would be careful. I'm not trying to frighten ya or anything, but this is the weirdest thing I've ever seen, and I've seen some bizarre sh—stuff!" With that, he held a lovely box of long-stemmed something out to me and left.

It seemed strange that a black satin ribbon held the box closed. It would have been a sweet presentation, but the ribbon's color alerted me that sweetness had nothing to do with what I held in my hands. I looked carefully around the property before hurrying back inside. Most of our guests were either outside or in their rooms. Still, with great stealth, I rushed to our suite and closed the door. My hands shook from all the drama. Carefully, I opened the box. Inside, nestled in black tissue, was a dozen black roses.

Hurrying to my computer, I Googled the meaning of black roses. What I found scared me: "The black rose, because it symbolizes death and passing away, also indicates a major change or upheaval in the future."

That was bad enough, but when I saw the card, I fell into the closest chair.

"If ya see a red-haired girl, well, ye'll know the end is near."

Who are ya? Why do ya hate us? Is this my end? That was my thought as I collapsed into my lavender wing-back chair.

Chapter Twenty-Seven

Time ticked past without much drama. Before I knew it, Christmas was upon us once again. Life had established a gentle flow except for; lately, the strange events that made little sense caused deep alarm.

Alladale was plastered all over the internet. Our reservation numbers had quadrupled since opening. I felt exhausted at the busy pace we set.

Our lodge had never looked prettier. With the passing of five years, we now decorated gloriously for the birth of a small baby who lived long ago. Each year, we celebrated Christmas in the same way but added a few new things. The result, to me, was perfection.

Max and Elizabeth had visited for this year's Christmas with their four children. They started a tradition of visiting each year before the grand season so they could return home to celebrate in the golden house. Both of the elder Reids had passed away. Thom and I had yet to go back to Charleston.

Ol' Sissy Smothers won't be liking this. Still not a chance of getting us to allow her to attend a Reid funeral. That thought made me laugh. *Momma had no idea the number of times we whispered her words throughout the years.*

Natasha was busily preparing dinner for a full house while Thom cut wood outside. With Christmas music echoing through the bright halls of Alladale, I finished wrapping presents. The staff would help us close down the lodge for January and February. It usually made me sad to cross off another year from my calendar, but this year, I felt tired and looked forward to a quiet time with my husband and the beautiful Alladale.

The entire staff would be gone this year. Usually, Pieter-Paul and Natasha stayed with us. This year both had requested time with their families. Pieter-Paul would return to his Dutch home while Natasha planned an extended visit with her Maltese family. Although I felt excitement at Thom and I roaming the lodge in peace, there was a bit of anxiety about remaining isolated for so long. That strange feeling that something was about to happen hung over me. Even though there were few overt threats against us, now and then, something would happen to remind us of the fact that we had an enemy.

Often, there would be a day of constant phone calls but no caller on the other end of the line. Two weeks ago, I had received another box of long-stemmed roses. A different young man delivered them. Roberto was chatty and friendly as he handed me the smart-looking white box tied with a shiny red bow.

Again, my hands shook as I carried the box with trepidation into the warm house. I laid it on the window table. What a relief when I opened the box to find a dozen bright red roses; they looked gorgeous. Inside, a small card was tucked into the white tissue waiting for me. By that time, my hands had stopped shaking.

The roses are red, Caroline, no need to fear, I had told myself. Yet, when I opened the little envelope, the card, in bold, brash letters, said:

"If ya see a red-haired girl, well, ye'll know the end is near."

Slumping back into my lovely lavender chair, I stared at the little card. "Can we have no peace from your nastiness? We don't even know who ye are! Why do ya hate us?" This insanity had been going on for too long.

Thom entered as I cradled my head in my hands, which now shook again, dramatically this time. "Aye, more black flowers, hey?"

"No, these are red, and they're gorgeous. I refuse to throw the beauties away. Instead, I'll proudly display them on the large round table in the lobby. It's pretty obvious that someone plans on continuing this intimidation, but for how much longer?"

Another year had speedily passed in our lives. It seemed the older we became, the faster our days flew by. Gloom filled my soul, but Christmas always made me sad. Not the real reason, but the realization that we were a year older. Plus, I still missed my family so much, especially at this time of the year.

"Thom, maybe we need a vacation. Let's plan to close the lodge and return to Charleston immediately after Christmas. What do ya say?"

"Aye, sounds like a good idea. I would love to visit the gold house and see those wee redheaded little ones running down the hall like Max and I once did. We should check on the wedding-cake house anyway."

We had arranged for Josey's daughter to live there and keep it afloat for us.

"Aye, we should. Ya know, I feel guilty keeping it, but I can't sell it. There's something in my head that says not to let it go."

Thom nodded. We looked at each other when we realized it might not be a good idea to leave the nature reserve unmanned.

"Duncan loves it here. Since business is slow this time of year at his hotel, I bet he'll agree to stay here." Thom referred to the Bunchrew Hotel as Duncan's because he received a promotion to the Manager position two years ago.

Duncan had finally fattened up a little. The extra weight looked good on him. He frequently used our gym and walked all over the property. He loved Alladale as much as we did.

"Aye, I'll check with him this evening." We planned on meeting him, Malcolm, and Molly to exchange gifts this evening at Duncan's hotel.

Our favorite little table in the back of the dining room had remained reserved for weeks. During the winter months, Duncan closed his hotel, as did we. He probably would look forward to time away. Our decision already provided me with peace, and excitement grew at the thought of returning to Charleston for a while.

"Ya know, it's hard to believe that we've been here for five years. Have I aged much? Don't lie, Thom."

"Aye, ya have, ye's an old woman. I don't know how I put up with ya." He sweetly kissed my right cheek as he spun me around. "We'll know when we're old when I'm unable to do this and one or two other things." His grin was wicked.

"Aye, ye think so?" I kissed him hard on the mouth.

After a quick shower, Thom and I headed to the hotel. The back of the car held two unique gifts for our beloved friends. I hoped they would be pleased. I located an original book signed by a famous author about the Battle of Culloden for Duncan. Molly and Malcolm would love the fragrant fruit cake from our chef as well as a gorgeous vase for their foyer. Both of the gifts were wrapped in beautiful heavy golden foil with bright red ribbons. Little clusters of natural berries peeped from the heavy wrappings.

"A penny for yer thoughts, Caroline, the belle of Charleston," I smiled. It had been a long time since my husband had called me that.

"Aye, the old belle," I returned his grin.

The Bunchrew House Hotel filled with guests, as did Alladale. We hurried inside; the wind blew fiercely. Dark clouds overhead threatened snow.

"Threats everywhere," I whispered to myself.

Inside, the scene was gay. The sweet aroma of a fire burning and the sight of natural winter Scottish greenery grouped in pretty bunches, such as seed heads, catkins, and ornamental bark, delighted me.

"Thom, why have I never thought of using natural plant materials from the winter garden? Aren't they beautiful?"

Suddenly, I felt Molly's gentle arms enfold me close to her. I had never asked her about the fragrance she always wore because I loved it so much. I knew I would copy her, and that wouldn't be right. *How does she consistently emit the delightful Scottish smells of malt, pine, and peat?*

"Molly, ye smell like the ancient Caledonian pines after a gentle summer rain. I'm not goin' to ask ya to tell me the name of yer wonderful scent."

"Aye, many a lass has tried to pry it from my lips, but I refuse. Besides, if I tell ya, I'll have to kill ya."

Those words sent a shudder down my very soul. When I turned, her eyes blazed with a fire I had never seen before. She looked angry and unhappy with me. It gave me pause.

Quickly, she grabbed me. "Ya know, I love ya." Her gay laughter sounded inappropriate.

I could only nod, but suddenly I wasn't so sure she did love me. Had I become paranoid because of the threats? The familiar words about a red-haired girl came briefly to my mind.

While our friends unwrapped our gifts, I observed Molly. She smiled with such love at me. *Is she my friend?* Duncan promised to bring our presents at a later time. Malcolm and Molly surprised us with a massive copper pot that would shine from the old kitchen shelf, which had remained empty for five years as I searched for the perfect object to display.

Chapter Twenty-Eight

The beauty of Alladale, shining in the night as she waited for Christmas, her big day, made me cry when we returned home. She never smelled as sweetly or reflected her beauty as brilliantly as she did when dressed in her Christmas best. The staff had helped the professional crew deliver boughs of pine, pine cones, and all sorts of natural red berries. Bright red bows with long, red streamers peeked from branches of fresh herbs and shrubs that looked breathtaking indoors. Mingling with the indigenous plants were rare white orchids. Those beauties reflected the red color of Christmas from within vast, creamy flowers. They peeped at guests with splashes of red in their centers. It all came together beautifully.

Thom had begun to labor on the two cottages, so he remained swamped with work. There wasn't enough time to complete them this year, but he planned to finish one as soon as spring burst forth the next year. Our estimated time for the completion of the entire estate was ten years. The first five had been glorious, except for the spread-out, weird, threatening events.

Hopefully, all that's over! I pray that the next five aren't so dramatic.

"Okay, my belle of Scotland, all the reservations are made. We should arrive in Charleston on January 5 and stay for two months."

"I'm excited. Just the thought of seeing little Caroline Emma thrills me. Maybe she can spend long summers here in Scotland when she's older."

"What about her brothers? Ya can't show favoritism, ya know?" He tousled my hair as Josey once had.

"Aye, they'll all be here with us."

Even our staff glowed in anticipation. The young people were all excited about visiting their homes for a much-deserved break. The thought of being away from Alladale for so long caused a pang of guilt in me, but Duncan had quickly accepted our offer to live here during our absence. Malcolm and Molly vowed to check on him. Lately, the lad bragged about a girlfriend that we had yet to meet. He kept promising to bring her soon, but that had never happened.

I never mentioned to Thom that I had suspected our dear friend, Molly, of being the red-haired girl in the strange messages. He would have called me paranoid. Still, I didn't feel quite the same around her. It had occurred to me that might be the purpose of all this craziness. Perhaps, someone wanted to drive me insane by making me paranoid. A vacation with my family was what I needed.

During this Christmas at Alladale, each of our guests was a repeat visitor. I loved it when guests returned because it felt like they were voicing approval for Alladale and us. All of these guests were easygoing; none of them were high-maintenance.

We felt relaxed but excited about our upcoming break. My husband and I had worked so hard these past five years. The big day, Christmas, was only one day away. Two days later, all the visitors would leave. Then, with the staff, I would begin to take down the Christmas joy for another year. We planned to depart on January 1 and enjoy an extended visit to Savannah before driving to Charleston. Thom and I appreciated the contrast between Savannah and Charleston. They were similar coastal towns yet very different.

A gentleman from Poland smiled sweetly at me. "Um, excuse me, Mrs. Reid, I'm wondering if I might get the recipe from Natasha for that à la Chateaubriand we enjoyed last night? It was exquisite."

Another guest, a woman from Spain, gently touched my hand. "Great meal, the other night, Mrs. Reid, do you think Natasha might share her secret for those delicious potatoes?"

The sound of an American voice gave me pause. "Mrs. Reid, we were wondering if we might reserve a cart to explore deeper into the forest today."

"Aye, where ya from?" I looked into deep blue eyes the color of the summer sky.

"My husband and I hail from the northern US. Did you ever hear of Minnesota?" I smiled and gave a little time to share my history.

We loved it when locals took time from a busy schedule to visit us. "We want to tell you how beautifully decorated Alladale appears this year. We don't live that far away and would like to hire your decorators. Do you have a card for them, dear?"

This pattern of questions and pleas for help had become my life, but I loved it. Seeing the smile on the face of someone who came to me with expectations that I could provide peace and relaxation had begun to feel natural. Even without our conservation work and the reintroduction of endangered species, I thought we gave back to those around us each day.

Thom continued to work tirelessly to bring back the wolves. That had become his mission. Each roadblock only increased his determination to accomplish this noble act. Daily, we achieved more publicity for our cause. Although many failed to support our efforts, it seemed more people did. They were stepping forward and helping champion our goal. It wasn't easy.

The past few days had been free from the intimidating harassment against us. I hoped that the worst was over. *Maybe, whoever committed such scary and unneeded threats had given up or decided we weren't worth the effort.* I hoped that was the case. There had been no more sightings of the silver-haired man who uttered his strange words each time he had seen me. Still, when I was around Molly, I no longer felt the love and security from her that I had once felt. Something changed between us, but she never mentioned it, nor did I.

Max phoned on Christmas morning with his clan. They were very excited about our visit. He had the wedding-cake house cleaned and polished, and the garden immaculately groomed for our arrival. We enjoyed a long chat. Then I phoned Josey's daughter, Tanya, who lived in the rooms inside Josey's little apartment. We looked forward to her presence in the wedding-cake house, not just when we returned for the two months but for the rest of her life. Tanya now occupied the little apartment at the foot of the stairs. Someone in her family had worked for mine for generations. They weren't employees; they were family. Tanya had always resembled Josey and was as sweet in her manner, but no one could take my Josey's place. For a moment, I sat in the lavender chair, thinking about my departed friend and surveying the lake from the large, slightly open window. I noticed an object lying on the shore near the water. It looked odd.

The temperature outside was brisk, but I needed a little exercise. I sauntered toward the object. As I walked, I pulled the heavy Original Irish Aran sweater that matched the one Duncan gave Thom around me. *What is that?* I touched it with my foot. It was a dead bird. I didn't recognize this species of duck, but something didn't seem right. Kneeling beside it, I saw a piece of rope around the neck with a bit of paper attached. I removed it. Scrawled in large letters:

"The same thing waits for you, Caroline! Leave Alladale!"

When I bent closer, I saw the duck's neck was broken. Someone had choked the life out of it. I thought I might be sick.

No, you coward, I'm not leaving. I won't even tell Thom about this. I don't want him to cancel our plans. Who would do this?

I hurried inside; I asked Innes to remove the dead bird. Before long, I completely forgot it, or I denied it by blocking it from my mind.

Yes, I desperately needed a respite from this craziness.

Chapter Twenty-Nine

"What a wonderful Christmas! I love the thought of getting married in Charleston next summer. Everyone keeps telling me that I'm weird for tying the knot in a strange place, but I see it as very romantic!" Molly's melodic voice touched my heart because of the friendship we once had.

Molly and Malcolm kissed as they enjoyed a lovely meal at the hotel the day after Christmas. Duncan was on the phone with his new girlfriend, whom we had yet to meet.

"Caroline, ya both are so kind to invite us to marry in yer wedding-cake house. I can't wait to see it. All these years, ye've talked about how special it is! Well, here's special." She kissed Malcolm again.

"Don't ya worry about not having a friendly crowd of people to celebrate yer day of blessing. We can provide a 'packed-house.' It's guaranteed."

Molly glowed at Thomas, but something was still very wrong between Molly and me. The fear of appearing paranoid from the escalating acts of intimidation against me prevented me from sharing my worries with my husband. *Whoever was doing this did not aim the attacks at him, only me; all of these threats involve only me.*

Duncan briskly approached us. He looked pale and was shaking. "I can't believe she did this!" He looked like he might burst into tears.

I hugged him before I helped him to the chair he had earlier occupied. He explained that the girl he thought he loved had just ended their relationship. "I know it sounds fast, but I was going to give her an engagement ring this spring. I guess I won't be doing that."

When I pressed him for a reason, it became obvious that it involved me. He glanced at me then quickly lowered his eyes.

"Caroline, ye aren't going to like this. I hate it for both of us." He got up and walked away but quickly returned, appearing more composed. "She's telling everyone that I continue to see ya on the side, Caroline, and that she walked in on us as we were, uh, ye know. Of course, it's a lie, Mr. Reid." He paled when he glanced at my husband.

"Aye, young Duncan, I know it's not true. Who is this girl? Why would she do such a thing? Ya do know that she never cared for ya, don't ye, lad?"

"Aye, I do now. The name isn't important, but it's Olivia. She's from a neighboring village and is my age. We're both young, I know that, but I truly believed that we were in love. Oh, how could she do this? All I've ever wanted was to have a relationship like the four of ya. I feel, once again, like an outsider. I'm always tagging along. I feel humiliated." He hung his head. I thought I saw a tear slide down his cheek.

We all attempted to comfort him but realized he would need time to heal.

Then a hotel patron walked past our table and paused. "Aye, Duncan, lost ye little lass, have ya? Well, I guess ya have bigger fish to fry." He laughed as he strolled away but not before staring rudely at Thomas and me. Others around us laughed but lowered their eyes when I stood.

"Ya believe this garbage? Do ye think I would do this sort of thing? I've lived among ye for over five years. Now, do ya really think that I would carry on with this young man behind the back of my husband?" Anger, such as I had never known, overtook me.

Thomas gently pulled me back into my chair. "Caroline, ya don't owe an explanation to anyone. If they believe this, which I doubt, then ye and Duncan can't change their minds. Don't ya stoop to their level. Ya stand up, my beautiful lass, for I love ya, and I know the truth. It's Duncan that I feel sorry for with his young age and all."

Molly touched the young man's cheek with a tender touch. Our young friend could stand no more and broke from the table and hurried away.

"I know, it's selfish of me, but do ya think he'll still stay at Alladale while we take our break? What if he refuses to leave here now?" Fear descended as I realized how important this trip had become to me. Thom kissed me and assured me that Duncan would never do that.

"Thomas, ye know how emotional he is. I fear that he will refuse to stay at Alladale, living alone and isolated. I think he looked forward to having his girlfriend with him there. Now, why would she do this?"

We discussed that Olivia must never have cared for our boy at all. What a terrible thing for Duncan to be hurt by his first love. My heart broke for him, but my own situation looked doomed. Molly managed to create a diversion by talking about her upcoming marriage to Malcolm.

As we settled down and finished our roasted duck and potatoes, several people meandered past, giggling. Poor Duncan would face this each day because he worked as the Manager of this famous place. His situation was direr than mine because he might lose his position over it.

After we said our goodbyes to Molly and Malcolm, Duncan walked toward us. "Thom, Caroline, I hate to do this, but I can't stay at Alladale for two months alone. My family thinks the isolation could be dangerous. They think that I'm too young for this much responsibility. My uncle says it's not because of Olivia but that he fears for me. I am pretty stressed out right now. Ya know that I'm sorry to do it. Can't ya just board up Alladale and hire security?" With no further explanation, he rushed away.

All of my pent-up frustration and fear burst out of the cage I had built for it. Tears streamed from my eyes as I shook with disappointment and, for the first time, real fear. Thom looked surprised. I was always the rock, the one dealing with death, betrayal, untold stress, and threats of violence. He gently shielded me as he guided me outside, away from the whispers and stares. I remembered seeing Duncan standing alone with a look of amazement that I had succumbed to emotion.

"Now, listen to me, Caroline. We will follow our earlier plans. Alladale will survive. Don't fear."

"It's just that I need to see little Caroline Emma. She probably doesn't know that I exist. I don't want to be like Uncle Robert. Ya know, someone who never visits or shows any concern for her. I know ya mean well, Thomas, but we can't leave Alladale. There's an incident that I never shared with ya. Things have escalated lately."

My husband's strong arms enfolded me, but I realized he was unable to fix this. *How can we leave our home? A maniac who threatened to harm me wouldn't hesitate to destroy Alladale.* Thom started the car for warmth, and he demanded that I share what I meant by "escalation."

Calmly and with no emotion, I confided the most recent incident of the dead bird. Now, it was my husband who turned pale.

He stared off into the distance. "Aye, yer right, we can't leave now. Alladale is too vulnerable. Ye and I must stay and try to draw this person out. He will make a mistake, and we can expose these cowardly acts and this weakling who has made ya life so hard. I promise ye, as soon as we discover this weakling's identity, we'll leave for the States and spend a long visit with our families. I know that yer disappointed. I am as well."

He hugged me. That beloved smell of pine and freshness soothed my spirits, but I couldn't stop the tears. They fell for such a long time that I thought they might never stop. Once I had shared the latest threat, I felt vulnerable. Now, I came to terms with its meaning. It appeared that I had more than one person trying to destroy me. Never in my life had I experienced such fear. We drove home in silence.

The day of our expected departure came and went. We kissed our staff goodbye as they hurried away without a care. I envied their freedom. Thom and I looked at each other as the last of our team, Pieter-Paul, rushed out to his car.

The sound of the closing door failed to create panic but peace. I took Thom's hand as we walked to the drawing-room. A fire burned; the flames lightened the early darkness.

"We are finally alone." Thom smiled.

"Really, we're always alone, aren't we? I mean, when we're born, we travel that route alone, and when we die, we must do it alone. It's always just us and God."

We sat on the sofa and stared out the window. For hours, we remained in an embrace.

Finally, Thom spoke. "I think that tomorrow, we need to visit the local police and tell them everything. This situation is spiraling out of control. Ya know, we should have done it much earlier. We're now isolated. Would ya feel better if we checked into the hotel for a while?"

I reminded him that they would close soon. Plus, if we did that, why not go to Charleston? We had created a dangerous situation by not addressing this earlier, though it had been easier to avoid dealing with it and not facing the facts.

"What will we do?"

He smiled. "We wait, but we must be smart. Don't ever come inside or go outside without locking the door and arming the security system. Don't ya ever leave without telling me where yer going. In fact, don't ya ever leave without me. I'm now your constant companion."

"Aye, ye've always been such," I kissed him.

"Aye, but even more so now. This isn't the time to behave recklessly, Caroline. We can't know the intentions of this crazed person or persons. No telling how far they might go to scare us. I believe someone is tryin' to make us sell Alladale. There's someone out there who doesn't know us and the fact that we are fighters. We don't run!"

His words caused the Scottish spirit to rise in me. That warrior spirit from long ago rose with a fierce rush. With determination and fearlessness, I agreed. *No, we won't back down! Maybe, once we had alerted the police, they would help us devise a plan.* Our security system was state-of-the-art with cameras surrounding us— what a perfect place to draw out a coward who intimidated a woman.

Who would do such a thing? Why? For hours we discussed our plight. We vowed to use every precaution as we moved forward for the next two months. We couldn't afford to become lax or fearful. Instead, we would discover the instigator of this madness and make him pay. I couldn't help but think or make *her* pay. *Is it you, Molly?* I thought I would break if I discovered that it was.

The sunset was dramatic. We shared a glass of champagne as we discussed future dreams for our beloved Alladale. We would never run from her. There wasn't room for quitters in this glorious land of legends about pirates and Vikings, certainly not from a Reid or Corbett.

The night sounds that I loved echoed over the glens. The cry of a distant owl made me aware that we weren't alone after all. All the animals we loved surrounded us. *Perhaps, the remote call we heard someday might be that of a wolf, claiming his spot in this ancient land?* Never again would we allow greed to destroy something as majestic as this land. Thom and I would fight against actions that might further damage this place, the other country we loved.

"Aye, Scotland, yer fight is now ours. Ya don't struggle alone."

Together, we kneeled by the open window, which overlooked the scene we loved the most. The blazing sun fell from the sky, and darkness overtook us.

"Dear God, we aren't alone. We need ya, and so does this place."

Again, we looked out into the darkness. *Does someone watch us?* I no longer feared not at all. I was ready to fight.

Chapter Thirty

The faintest light shined into my darkened room. It was no longer chilly but freezing. My teeth chattered. As the sun softly peeked into the pretty lavender chamber, a faint glimmer raced through my mind. "I understand it all," I spoke with great effort into nothingness.

"At last, I remember all the memories of my past and can weave them together. Still, I am unable to figure out who has created such suffering for me. I know that my Thomas is dead. Most likely, when he opened the door. That hit on his head was powerful. Whoever designed this scheme is brilliant but evil." Fear caused the bile to rise in my throat, or was this a complication from dehydration?

Clearly, I sensed that my death was near. I was almost sure the third night had passed so that I wouldn't live much longer. Although I wasn't sure how long I had been here, the awareness that my body was shutting down had moved me toward these final memories from my past.

Dr. Lafferty peered into my eyes again as he lifted my head with his index finger. For the first time in my young life, I felt fear as I considered that my pediatrician must be more than just a doctor. *Is he capable of seeing the future?* I thought those silly thoughts at that time. My thoughts today did not appear so foolish. *Someone has wanted to kill Thom and me. And they have succeeded with Thom.*

On this early morning, I worried about what I had learned from Dr. Lafferty so long ago. In the good doctor's office all those years ago, I had discovered that no matter how hard I fought and tried to control my future, there would be times that I would be unable to do so. This day was surely such a time. The outcome was out of my reach.

Thom couldn't survive the blows, how can I? If he was unable to resist this evil beast who is set on destroying us, how can I? I now remembered those last few hours before I woke up shackled to this bed. *Maybe forcing myself to relive significant moments of my life did help me to decipher these final chapters.* I couldn't be sure. I wasn't sure of anything except that God was the only one here with me. I lifted my eyes to Him, and the final memories flooded my mind.

It was 2 a.m. I had glanced at the clock when a jangling sound woke me. Thom's arm held me tightly. The phone destroyed our peace.

"Who would phone at such an ungodly hour? Something must be wrong." Quickly, he rose from beside me. I missed his arm, that wall of protection from the world.

"What? Ye're who? Oh, yes, yes, of course, in my driveway? Sure, that's not a problem, I'll take care of him right away. Okay, don't worry. I'll instruct him to phone ya as soon as he's safely here. Don't worry. I'm on my way." Thomas pecked my cheek. He appeared distracted.

"Caroline, that was Duncan's uncle. I'm still half asleep, but it seems the young lad has lost his mind. The uncle says he sat up late into the night talking with Duncan, who was crying and threatening to kill himself over the actions of that lass, Olivia. At the last moment, Duncan ran to his car and thundered away.

"A few hours ago, he called his uncle. The young lad hit something in our driveway and has injured himself. Duncan might have been drinking. Don't ask me why he came here. Probably, he was so distraught that he was unable to think clearly. I'm going to find him and bring him here. Together, we'll make sure he's okay. Before he left his home, Duncan screamed that we're the only ones who understand him. Come on, Caroline. Ya need to go with me. I'm not leaving ya here alone."

"Thomas, that's crazy, let me start a pot of coffee. Ya hurry on and get him. Poor Duncan, hurry, Thomas, he needs us. Ye'll be here on the property, in the driveway, and only away for a few minutes."

"Aye, I guess yer right. Follow behind me and lock the door."

I followed him down the stairs. When he opened the door, a strange man waited. He hit Thom over the head with a heavy object. I couldn't tell who it was. My husband's eyes met mine as he fell hard on the threshold of Alladale. This man, who looked vaguely familiar, rushed into the room. Using unnecessary force, he grabbed me. I felt his hatred. *No, I'll never live through this,* I thought.

This intruder appeared to know his way around our home. He half-dragged, half-carried me to our bedroom. He took shackles out of the backpack he wore and fastened my hands and feet to our bed. Anger and profanity spewed from his evil mouth. I felt worthless and afraid. He secured the metal much too tightly.

"You see, I don't want you to die yet. It will give me such joy to watch the light slowly fade from your eyes. The amazing thing is how much you resemble *her.* Oh, how I hated her!" He pulled on the restraints with great force one last time.

"Let's open your window so that the cold air will make you suffer a little more once this fire fades. I'm not building and lighting it for your warmth, but to make you feel more pain. In the beginning, you'll be so hot that you'll pray to die. Soon, you will plead for the heat as you freeze."

My eyes strayed to the pitcher sitting by my bed.

"Ah, yes, the pitcher, brilliant strategy, don't you think? You'll question if there was water in it and if it might have prolonged your life? I'm so sorry that I dropped it; how foolish and careless. It's just that I've looked forward to this day for so long." The crazed laughter from this maniac ricocheted inside my beloved room.

"Thom? Have you killed Thomas? Oh, please, no, kill me, but don't hurt him! You hate me. Why hurt him?"

"You still don't get it, do you? Because you loved him so much. When I choke the life out of you, in a little while, like that duck, remember? Then I shall take possession of Alladale. All the things I've done, it's all about *this* place. For so long, I have schemed to obtain it. When I finally was able to make it all work, you and your husband derailed my plans and bought it. You're now paying for your greed." He smiled, turned on his heel, and hurried away.

Drained from the harshness of these last three days, at least I thought it had been that long, there was nothing left in me.

"Don't worry, Thom. I'm coming soon." I passed out.

"So, I finally remember. The man who hit Thom on the head has left me here to die." My body shook from the extreme cold and trauma. Once again, I passed out, but there were no pleasant recollections to soothe me. There was nothing. It felt as if I drifted over my bed.

"Wake up, girlie. The fun begins!" Hard slaps landed on my face, they revived my exhausted body. Standing by my bed was the silver-haired man with the cane. He laughed. My vision was extremely blurred, and my head hurt.

"You! All the time, I suspected it was you! Who are you?"

Evil taunts and jeers filled the room from this old stranger's mouth. Suddenly, he stood upright. Each time I had seen him, I had noticed that his shoulders slumped with age. Now, he stood straight as an arrow. He ripped the silver hair from his head. This person wasn't old, not at all. Using the wig, he wiped off the makeup he wore. He threw his cane to the side.

"I hope you realize the compassion I have shown to you. I could have killed you when you were fresh and had a little spunk left but decided to let you wilt. Now, you don't need to fight so hard. Remember the pretty lavender flowers? Clever, wouldn't you say? The way I allowed you to observe the death of the pretty little flowers. Just like you, they had to die. This entire plan has been skillfully thought and delivered. How horrible to have days to

217

consider your blessed life while realizing it would end soon—all of those little nuances that most people can never enjoy. You, Caroline, had it all. Your precious momma saw to it. Didn't she? How sad that I have the power to rip it all from you. Have you enjoyed your little 'walk down memory lane?' I knew you would fight to remember your privileged life. Not so special now, is it? Welcome to my life because of your mother. I've endured so much pain.

"My companion and I have different plans for your little nature reserve than those of you and your handsome husband. We're going to build a huge hotel and develop your beautiful land with tiny houses. If you'd lived to see it, you would have cried, no wolves, no bears, no lynx, none of your pets. Our plan is massive housing that will rape your beloved land and devour its nature.

"Remember the duck? Well, that was just the beginning of death for your mighty schemes. Think about this. It will end soon. You lost your husband, soon, your good friend, and this place you loved so much. Then, we'll take the wedding-cake house that you rambled on about all the time."

"What? The wedding-cake house? How do you know it? What friend will I lose? I don't understand. Please, just finish me. My life is nothing without Thom. I don't need to suffer anymore. I'm ready; what good is my life anyway?" I stiffened my body in preparation for whatever he had planned for me.

"Oh, I'll let you know when you don't have to suffer anymore. You still don't understand. Caroline, you have no control over this. You and your mother always thought, because of your extreme beauty, that you could control everything. You can't. Now, *we* are in control."

"We? Who are the others?"

"You don't get to ask questions. It will all unfold soon enough but at *my* speed. I have control. I've always been in control. Here is the answer to one of your questions."

Gloating, he pranced from the room. Moments later, Duncan entered. His paleness was frightening.

"Duncan, you're a part of this? I don't understand. Is Thomas really dead? Did you kill him? Why Duncan? Why?"

Before he could answer, the stranger strolled into the room. "Him? He's unable to kill a fly. No, surely, you don't think he could kill one as strong as your Mr. Reid? You're foolish if you do. I claim the honor of killing that brute."

I cringed at his words.

"See, old Duncan here is so gullible. When I encouraged him to write the article about how much he respected and cared for you, and I published it in The Post and Courier, all that played right into my plans. The way this will end is that the good lad killed your husband so that he could have *you*. When you denied him, the weakling turned and killed you. Everyone knows how weak and emotional the boy is. Then he killed himself. He's so pathetic.

"It may be a little hard for those who know the lad to accept, but the general population will bite into it because it fuels their need for lust and deceit. Half the town already thinks you're a slut and would do just about anything to fill your wicked sexual appetite.

"Why you would choose someone like Duncan might create questions, but they will accept it. All of you will go down as lustful, greedy monsters. I only had one little circumstance that I couldn't predict. Come on in here, Missy."

Again, he laughed when he saw the horror on my face as Molly entered. She looked paler than Duncan. Molly shook her head but continued to walk slowly toward me. *What is she trying to say?*

"Your good friends presented a problem for me. Two days after I left you here, Malcolm and Molly began to poke around. I had a friend posted at the entrance to Alladale once I had killed Thomas. By the way, his body lies at the bottom of your lake. Sort of ironic, don't you think? That very place the two of you loved so much now holds him? Think of all the years you toasted your success and commitment for each other, which ironically enfolds the corpse of the one you loved the most.

"Oh, dear Mr. Reid, I'm sorry I had to kill you, but our plans would never come to fruition as long as you lived." He talked to Thom as he faced the open window. *This maniac is unhinged!*

He pushed Molly toward me. "Caroline, this stranger has killed Malcolm. I've looked everywhere. They killed him as well as Thom."

Her tears looked real, and I realized all my doubts about her were unfounded. She and Malcolm had tried to help Thom and me.

"Yes, in a few moments, Duncan will stab you until you die, pretty Caroline. Then he'll cut his wrists. Such a feminine way to die, but he always was such a weakling. Now, weren't you, dearest nephew?" Again, his crazy laughter filled the somber room.

"You're Duncan's uncle? Why would you do all of this?"

"And they called you a prodigy. You aren't smart at all. Just like your Momma and all women, you're a conniving slut. Molly, you could have gone about your simple life. Now I guess you will indeed be able to visit the wedding-cake house for your wedding! You'll just be marrying a new groom!" He laughed at our looks of confusion.

"If only you and your nosey husband would have left things alone. A few times, you came close to discovering my plan. Right at the end, you and Malcolm were only a hairsbreadth from unearthing the entire plot! We were forced to act more quickly than we liked."

"Again, why do you hate me so much?" My screams at this evil man only procured more laughter. I found all the ramblings challenging to follow.

"Caroline, it's not you that I despise, but you stand in place of your momma. That lying bitch left me standing at the altar and made a fool of me. For all of my life, the people of Charleston laughed at me while they slung condescending remarks my way. You now know how it feels. From the time of her betrayal, I dreamed of revenge. Well, it's revenge time!" Again, he gave his evil cackle.

"You poor, dumb woman. You never questioned Duncan about his last name. I always thought when he divulged it, you might be suspicious, but you were too stupid. Does the name ABERNATHY ring a bell? Think! I know that your organs are shutting down from dehydration, cold, starvation, plus maybe, a little shock, but you can surely identify me?

"I'm Jack Abernathy, the man your treacherous mother left standing like a fool at the altar. Do you get it now? The man who is best friends with your Uncle Robert? The two of us have been besties since childhood. We attended The Citadel together. Now, well, our friendship has turned to love. We are married. Come on in, 'Uncle Robert!'" Jack jumped up and down like a child.

To my shock, the man I detested most in this world strode into the room with his arrogant head held high. He kissed Jack on the mouth, then immediately spat in my face.

"Yes, niece, my lover, and I will now take all that you love. We hope your worthless parents can watch it all from wherever they are. I want them to witness every gruesome detail of your end. Everyone in Charleston spoke of your mother with such love and respect while chastising me for my actions.

"Our good friend, Judge Harrelson, who helped us create disastrous legal problems for your family, will, once again, help us. He is brilliant and will be able to tie up any loose ends. Our associate will be moving here, to Alladale, where he will join us in the ideal life. Maybe, with a new start, we'll be able to find the respect we've always deserved."

Jack and Robert pounded each other on the back in glee. They stood facing into the room, away from the doorway. Behind them, I saw a shadow pass in the bright early morning light. *Thomas, do you remain alive?* Joy filled my soul that he might be well and save us all.

Molly looked at me. I could tell that she had also seen the shadowy silhouette. *If it isn't Thom, does Jack have another person waiting to shock us with more of his evil plans?*

"We must admit ol' Molly here threw a wrench into our well-oiled scheme. At the last minute, Robert has solved this dilemma she has created. No one in Scotland knows of Robert. He plans to be the one who, with his true love, Molly, divulges what happened to you and your husband to the police. Your talk about a silver-haired man with a cane and those crazy words:

'If ya see a red-haired girl, well, ye'll know the end is near.'

"Everyone thought you were crazy. No one ever admitted to seeing this deranged old man because he quickly removed his mustache and straightened his shoulders. Everyone looked for a very old fellow, not someone fit like Jack. We took turns dressing the part of a deranged madman. It was such fun.

"As for Molly, we will keep her drugged for a short while. She will be a good girl, won't you, sweet Molly? You'll be able to live for a little bit. Eventually, you will profess to all your friends how this older, savvy American swept you off your feet. Just as Mark did to Caroline's slut of a mother. Dazzling plan, don't you agree? As you flit around Inverness, dear Molly, all suspicions of the strange circumstances surrounding Caroline's, Thomas's, and Duncan's deaths will magically dissipate.

"The disappearance of Malcolm, well, everyone will attribute it to another man who lost his direction because of a despicable woman. You are all that! They will think that Malcolm just walked away from the pain. At least that's what the gullible people will say. Before we finish with you, sweet Molly, we'll take you to the Charleston wedding-cake house. The one where you planned to marry Malcolm. So sad that didn't happen." Jack wiped his left eye as if removing a tear.

"You'll charm the town with your lithe body and adorable accent. The cute little Irish girl, so innocent, such a shame that late one night, after drinking too much, she fell down the steep stairs to her untimely death. You were all such heavy drinkers. Once again, you made our work easier.

"Robert and I are good at acting. The drama suits us. We can't wait to return to Charleston, where we'll sell the house that you adored, the shining white wedding-cake house. You have no more family, Caroline. Only your dear uncle Robert will stand in line for the inheritance. People will attribute the quick sale to Robert's grief over the loss of his sweet little Molly and his niece, Caroline. Once all of that is finished, Alladale, here we come! Delightful, don't you think?" He and his lover laughed.

Again, something moved behind the two men as they rejoiced over their apparent genius.

"Are the two of us not brilliant? All right, Duncan, I need you to stab Caroline. Remember, the harder and deeper the thrust, the faster your friend dies. We don't want to prolong things, now do we? Hasn't she suffered enough? Don't you worry. We won't expect you to slit your own wrists. Happily, we'll do it for you."

Duncan was unaware of the presence of someone hiding behind the door. Robert pushed the young boy forward.

"Be a man for the first time in your cowardly life." Jack's hatred and anger spewed forth. He handed a silver-handled knife to Duncan. It was polished and looked sharp.

"I won't do it. If you want Caroline dead, *you* kill her. You're right about me. I would never kill anything, but I'm not weak. You don't know what you're saying." He stood defiantly before his uncle Jack and Robert.

The mysterious figure behind them moved slowly. Finally, I recognized that face. It wasn't Thomas but Malcolm. Molly turned at that moment. I feared that her expression might change and alert the killers to his presence. But she was too smart. Like me, she maintained her cool and showed no emotion. Malcolm continued to inch forward. He was a large man, even stouter than Thom.

"Go ahead, lad, thrust the knife into that pretty chest. If you don't, we will, and when we kill you, you'll wish you had obeyed us."

Duncan began to back away. "No! I refuse to hurt her. I don't care what you do to me. You, Uncle Jack, are a despicable human being if you can be called human. You're an animal, a monster." He continued to move farther away. I was amazed that he didn't see Malcolm, who now stood only inches from Jack and Robert.

Suddenly, without warning, Duncan plunged the knife into his own chest. He gasped, and blood ran from his mouth. He fell against Molly—the flowing blood from his chest smeared her pink dress. Everything happened in slow motion. It felt surreal. I gazed into the brown eyes of that large form now standing mere inches from me.

With little sound, Malcolm grabbed Jack in a chokehold. The sound of the older man's neck snapped in the early morning quiet. When he saw what happened to his partner, Robert began to plead for his life. He promised Malcolm all sorts of things if he would let him live.

"Ye killed me best friend, did ye? Ye was goin' to hurt me girl here. Molly never hurt a fly. And now ye've as good as killed Duncan!"

"No, I didn't. Duncan killed himself. He was a weakling. We just put him out of his misery. It's okay. You'll see." Uncle Robert laughed loudly.

Malcolm grabbed him as if he were a limp doll and placed his head in the same chokehold that he'd used on Jack. He snapped Robert's neck without a drop of sweat falling from his brow. Afterward, he lovingly held Molly while I felt myself slipping from life. They stood together, staring.

"I guess you won, Uncle Robert," I whispered.

A bright light enfolded me into the arms of peace.

I'm gone, it's over, I thought.

Chapter Thirty-One

When I woke in the hospital, Molly sat by my bed, and her gentle voice soothed my fears. I knew I was highly sedated. It felt like I was floating, suspended in the air. The sensation was similar to the bright light of peace I had felt earlier.

Was that death? Did I almost die?

A doctor appeared at my bedside. Before he stepped out again, he explained that I had been as close to death as anyone he had ever seen.

"Don't try to speak, my dearest Caroline. All is well. Malcolm will be here soon."

"Thomas? Molly, did they really kill him?"

I saw her hesitate, and I knew she thought the truth might be too much for me. "I can take it, Molly. Please, I'm begging ya. I have to know."

"Aye, Caroline, they found his body, bound and weighted, yesterday at the bottom of the lake at Alladale. They say he died from blunt force trauma to the head, so he didn't drown. Duncan also died from his self-inflicted stab wound.

"Malcolm and I are fine, and so are ye. They say that ye'll be well enough soon to leave the hospital. Ye've been here for two days; they're bringing ya out of an induced coma because yer screams filled the hospital, and ya poor body needed to rest. They couldn't make ye stop. I'm so sorry."

Molly held her breath as though she feared I might begin to scream again. But I couldn't. My voice sounded hoarse, and my throat felt raw. After her explanation, I fell asleep.

Later in the day, when I woke, Malcolm waited with Molly.

I felt a little better. "Molly, I have a confession. Right before all this happened, I suspected ye were involved in a plot to harm me. Ya have to know this. I'm ashamed that I ever suspected ya of plotting against me. I hope that ye'll forgive me." The energy to speak those words was all I could muster.

"Aye, something had changed in yer eyes. I didn't know what it was, but I felt that ya no longer trusted me. Caroline, ya don't need to apologize to me. Ye've dealt with indescribable loss and drama over these last years. Malcolm and I want ye to know that we're here for ya. We'll stay with ya. Do ya want to come home with us to Allt? It means 'stream' ya know?"

I felt her gentle touch as she held my hand. "Can't I go home to Alladale?"

"Aye, we'll make sure ya go back when the staff returns. Malcolm will employ security to ensure yer safety. Aye, Caroline, eventually, but now, ya going to need care. We insist that ye come home with us to Allt."

I felt too weak to argue, but I nodded.

On March 1, I finally returned to my beloved Alladale after spending a few weeks with my friends. All the staff had returned, and together we prepared to open for another season. The crew had been with me so long that I thought of them as family. Their constant attention made me feel loved and protected.

Often, on a summer evening, I walked to the lake. I did it so frequently that Remi placed an Adirondack chair there for me. The peace that surrounded me at this place that I loved, healed me. Sometimes, I lifted a toast of champagne to my beloved husband. Without him, as much as I loved this place and our earlier dreams of restocking the wolves, my heart was too broken to continue. Those old dreams were too overwhelming.

Before long, another place called me. It wasn't the call of the wild but that of my beloved Charleston. Max and Elizabeth visited me; they had taken my husband's body back to the family cemetery months earlier.

"You need to come home, Caroline. Scotland held your dreams with Thomas, but he's gone now. Come home. Let us care for you. The children want to know their aunt. Little Caroline Emma has made great plans for the two of you. Let us take you home."

Max refused to leave until I agreed. Elizabeth had to return home without him. No matter how hard I tried to persuade him to return to Charleston, he refused to leave me. When he began to miss his family so much that it affected him, I knew I had to return with him, for both our sakes.

Malcolm and Molly sold their beautiful home, Allt, and purchased Alladale. Those dreams of ours, Thomas's and mine became theirs. They promised to continue the fight for the return of the wolves and other endangered species. A fire glowed in Malcolm's brown eyes when we stood together with Molly watching the sunset. I knew well that fire, which once burned in another set of chocolate eyes.

I no longer cried each time I thought of my husband. My grief would never leave me, but I learned to deal with the pain.

"Aye, Thom, I'm going home. Alladale will remain our home, but I need to move on to the next chapter. A new one calls to me — that of young feet running down the shiny halls of the wedding-cake house. I will be leaving a piece of me heart here at Alladale. In the rest of it, I will carry yer memory forever."

I stood proudly at the threshold of Alladale as Malcolm and Molly moved into our home. I handed the substantial key ring to Malcolm.

"It's yers now, my friends. Many people died trying to possess this place, but I believe she has a soul incapable of possession by mere man. Ya see, I think God lives here in Alladale. This place might be His second home. When He needs a change, maybe, He leaves heaven and comes here. How else can we explain such unparalleled beauty as this? Nowhere else are there sunsets like these.

"But my broken heart needs to let this place go. The two of you can teach yer children the importance of every species in nature's plan. Can't ya picture them being wed here in this beautiful place? Alladale is the perfect place for weddings, ya know."

"Aye, we do. We've been wonderin' how to tell ya that we have decided to be married at Alladale. I hope that we haven't hurt yer feelings. Will ya explain our decision to Max and Elizabeth? We plan on visiting all of ya at the wedding-cake house for part of our honeymoon. If that's still okay?"

Their news pleased me. How well I understood the power of this site, Alladale. Once I moved here, it felt impossible to abandon her. I wondered about the power that she held over those she loved. *Would she prevent their leaving? Like a jealous mistress, does she flaunt her power?* It seemed possible.

Max and I left Scotland later that same morning. We walked away from the handsome couple as the sun shined gently on an early spring morning. The sound of ducks and geese fussing in the background made me smile. I could now look at the lake and see its beauty again.

"I'm coming home, Thomas."

Still, I turned one more time for another look at my other love, Alladale. And as I turned, the door slowly closed.

"Well, Thom, it's time for a new chapter, a different adventure's callin'."

Max and I slowly walked away.

Chapter Thirty-Two

For the rest of my life, which I hoped wouldn't last long without my husband, Max, and Elizabeth surrounded me with their nurturing spirits. When I looked at them, I often thought of sweet Josey.

I woke at one point on that long trip back to Charleston as exhaustion ravaged my body. My head fell onto Max's shoulder and chest, and the front of his shirt was wet with my saliva. The next time I awoke, I felt such embarrassment, but it was nothing like what I had experienced earlier when I relieved myself numerous times in my bed. At that time, I had vowed never to be embarrassed again.

My vow had not lasted long. It must have been terribly uncomfortable for Max with my head resting on him. I supposed that he was as tired as I. He didn't seem to notice the giant wet spot on his shirt. For a second, I considered pouring a drink down his chest to explain it.

Caroline, you still have a sense of humor. How can you? I smiled at the thought.

Max opened his big brown eyes. He looked confused while considering how he ended up on a plane with me.

"Don't ya worry, Max, we'll be home to yer Elizabeth and yer little ones soon."

He smiled with a nod. When he saw the wet spot, he laughed. Gently, he wiped the remaining drool from my lips. We behaved like this for the rest of our lives. He and Elizabeth were my family. Their children were mine.

My life continued for over thirty years. I know because I'm still counting the years and how slowly they pass. Long, pleasant memories of my blond-haired handsome man fill my dreams instead of the flashes of thoughts that I once experienced.

I never figured out what that strange phrase,

"If ya see a red-haired girl, well, ye'll know the end is near" meant.

Most likely, it was a ploy to add confusion, setting me up to distrust Molly. We surely didn't need any more of that.

Months after I moved back into the wedding-cake house, I finally looked through years of photos, memories from Alladale. At the bottom of a box, I found an envelope that contained photos from our Open House celebration. Lovingly, I stroked the face of Thom and Daddy. At the back of the group, I noticed a man with a big smile, looking at the camera.

I studied his face and felt shocked to see Jack Abernathy among the guests who celebrated with us. For a few moments, nausea overcame me that he had the nerve to enter our home under the guise of friendship. His image was a little blurry, and only he looked out of focus in the picture. My hands began to shake as I looked at the man who took Thom and tried to kill me.

For weeks, I carried that picture around. I didn't know how to settle the emotions that churned in my soul about it. Then wise words rang through my troubled mind. It was as though Josey sat before me.

"Now, Miss Caroline, what would Jesus do?"

I immediately realized that it wasn't my place to find vengeance. I whispered, "Josey, I believe that Jesus would tell me to forgive him. Jesus would say that He and only He holds justice in His hands. I don't know if I can, but I'm going to try."

With those words, I sat down in the middle of the floor and cried as if my heart might break. For so long, I had carried my pain and grief. When I, at last, understood the magnitude of Jack and Robert's hatred, it became apparent that only God could understand what had driven them. I had no choice but to turn it over to the One who promised justice to His children. Suddenly, my burden felt lighter.

"Caroline, you don't have to do anything but let it go," I told myself.

After that, I cried for months. When I thought of Thomas, I wept. When I missed Alladale, I grieved. It took a very long time. At last, I understood the meaning of closure and its importance.

It also took me a long time before I could stay alone in my wedding-cake house. Tanya remained with me but offered little security. Max hired a man who stayed with us at night. The security guard remains at my door each evening.

Without much hesitation, I began to write. It had been years, and my creative side needed this outlet. My work became well-read, and my popularity both in South Carolina and Scotland soared.

"Oh, Daddy, Momma, Josey, and dearest Thomas, I wish you could see me. You all would be so proud!" No longer did I use the Scottish lilt.

The unsung hero of our misadventure had been the young Duncan Abernathy. My first book detailed his bravery as he courageously faced two cowards. His sweet face filled my dreams. His life was short and not very happy, but I prayed that he had found solace in the arms of Jesus.

"Jesus? Now, what would Jesus say about all of this?" I laughed as my Josey came to mind. *How many times had she asked me that phrase during my childhood?*

Her daughter, Tanya, has the same spirit. Each day, she makes me smile. She looks so much like her mother. The funny thing is that she goes through the Reid's trash every two days, as her mother did, and removes the flowers that Elizabeth's maid, Wanda, has thrown away. Thus, that little apartment still smells like chocolate mixed with the sweetness of flowers. I often pretend to have a problem so that I can visit her space.

All of us are old now. Max and Elizabeth are the proud grandparents of seven. I never missed not having my own children. My books are my children, although there are so many that I seem to have lost count.

Molly and Malcolm continue to live at Alladale. Each of their many visits to South Carolina brings such joy. Their son, Malcolm, the younger, has three little boys.

And what of Alladale, you ask? My beloved friends continue the fight to create a fenced/controlled wolf reserve to manage the red deer population. Malcolm, the elder, desires to create an ecological balance that existed before the rape of the land began in the name of progress. It hasn't happened yet, but as more people become aware of our environment's perils, I believe it will. My prayers remain with that land of silver mountains and the bluest of waters where my heart once awakened each day inside my beloved Alladale.

Because of Thomas Baxter Reid, I have been made painfully aware of the issues that face each country. In fact, our planet must work together to stop the many acts of destruction we commit each day against our environment. These damages can still be altered. Many of our past actions are reversible, but we must start now, today, in our quest to find solutions and work together. This threat is the greatest that Scotland's habitat face, whether it be the coast or my beloved Highlands. These climate changes will adjust downward the intricate ecological balances that allow plants and animals to grow and thrive.

Increasing ocean temperatures and ocean acidification are the most dramatic of the changes that are occurring. They are the primary catalysts for a rise in ocean levels and the loss of polar ice.

The good news is that Scotland has become a world leader in providing its electricity from renewables. As far back as 2017, the country created eco-friendly energy. About 68.1 percent of the entire amount of energy consumed in Scotland was provided by renewable sources, which was an improvement of 14.1 percent. This amount was an upgrade from 54 percent in 2016.

Yes, my husband and I were champions when we lived in Scotland. My adventure there is a bit of a legend. Who would have thought in that land of warriors and Vikings that one as nameless as I might be worth remembering? But it's really my Thom they refuse to forget. They allowed him to battle beside them for the reintroduction of species that have vanished.

When I'm not writing, I fight for the environmental issues impacting the United States: acid rain, overfishing, deforestation, so many causes. The main problems remain ozone depletion, greenhouse effect and global warming, desertification, deforestation, loss of biodiversity, and waste disposal.

Specific to Charleston is the rising sea level, which affects coastal wetland ecosystems in most areas. Such a problem creates habitat loss, seawater encroachment, flooding, and harm to Charleston's water quality. The fact that climate changes are both real and manmade clearly impacts South Carolina authentically and dramatically.

As more young people become aware of these delicate issues, I'm encouraged that there will be others who join this cause. It remains a certainty that Thomas would be fighting with me. Max, Elizabeth, Tanya, my entire family frequently accompany me to Washington.

Yes, I have had a full life, a blessed one. And sometimes, in the middle of the night, when I have an open window by my bed, I finally hear the call of the wild which Thom talked about so often. No longer do nightmares torment me.

Now, I have peace, but the cry of the wolf will forever hold my heart.